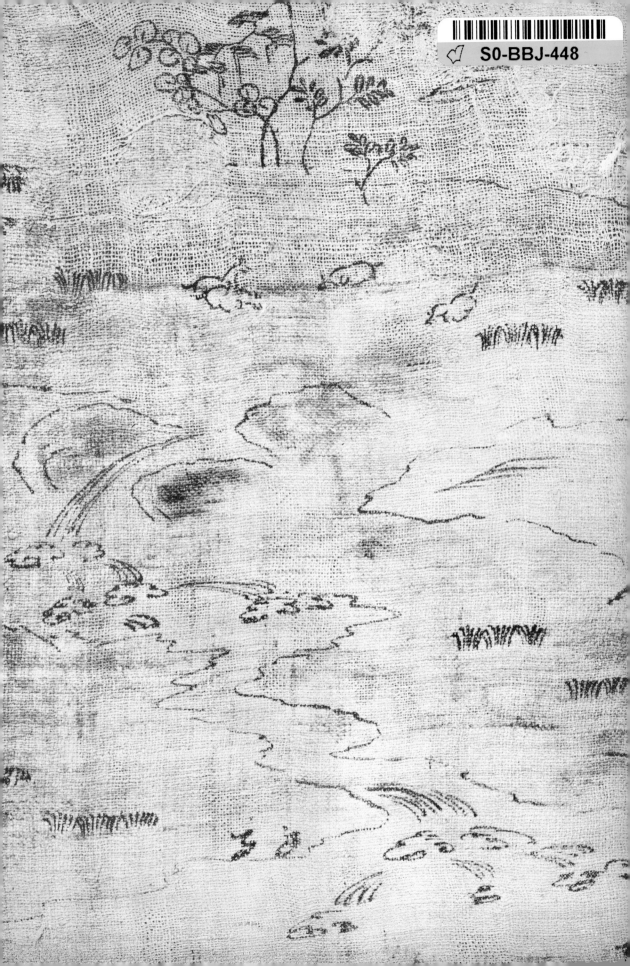

The Landscape Painting
of
China and Japan

ABOUT THE AUTHOR

Hugo Munsterberg was born in Germany, the son of the famous German Orientalist Oskar Münsterberg. He has lived in the United States since 1935, receiving his A.B. and Ph.D. degress from Harvard University, where he followed his father's footsteps by specializing in Oriental art, studying under Benjamin Rowland, Langdon Warner, and Laurence Sickman. After completing his doctoral thesis on Chinese Buddhist bronzes, he taught Oriental art first at Wellesley College and then at Michigan State College. He is now Professor of Art History at the International Christian University, Tokyo.

In addition to many articles and book reviews on the art and culture of China and Japan, he has published two books: *A Short History of Chinese Art* (1949) and *Twentieth Century Painting: 1900—1950* (1951). A new book by him dealing with the history of Japanese art is now in preparation and is scheduled to be published by the Charles E. Tuttle Company in 1956.

Autumn Landcape, traditionally ascribed to Emperor Hui Tsung

Hugo Munsterberg

The Landscape Painting

of

China and Japan

CHARLES E. TUTTLE COMPANY

Rutland, Vermont   Tokyo, Japan

Published by the Charles E. Tuttle Company
of Rutland, Vermont and Tokyo, Japan
with editorial offices at
15 Edogawa-cho, Bunkyo-ku,
Tokyo, Japan

First edition, June, 1955

WP66+
M928ℓ

Library of Congress Catalog Card No. 55-10624

Printed in Japan by
Toppan Printing Company, Tokyo
Frontispiece printed by Benrido, Kyoto
by arrangement with Heibonsha, Tokyo

TO MY MOTHER
WHO TAUGHT ME TO LOVE ART
AND TO THE MEMORY OF MY FATHER
OSKAR MÜNSTERBERG

ACKNOWLEDGEMENTS

It would be impossible to list all those who in one way or another have been of help to me in my study of Chinese and Japanese landscape painting, for this work has been possible only through the labors of my colleagues, both Western and Oriental. However I wish to acknowledge above all my indebtedness to my teachers at Harvard University, Professor Benjamin Rowland and Mr. Laurence Sickman, with whom I studied Chinese painting and Mr. Langdon Warner, under whom I studied Japanese painting.

No one working in this field can do so without drawing heavily upon the scholarship of Professor Osvald Siren whose books on Chinese painting and translations from Chinese texts have been of immeasurable help in my studies. The same may be said of the translations undertaken by Professor Alexander Soper and Miss Shio Sakanishi, and to them I wish to express my thanks for letting me quote from their writings.

I wish to thank the private collectors and museums who have been kind enough to permit me to draw upon their material for the illustrations in this book, especially Mr. John Pope of the Freer Gallery of Art in Washington, Mr. Robert Paine of the Boston Museum of Fine Arts, Mr. Laurence Sickman of the Nelson Gallery in Kansas City, Miss Hiroko Kojima of the National Museum in Tokyo, Miss Akiko Ueno of Bijutsu Kenkyujō, and Dr. Victoria Contag of the University of Mainz. Finally, I am deeply indebted to my wife, whose help and advice has been a tremendous asset throughout the writing of this book; it may indeed be said that it would not have been written without her aid and encouragement.

Hugo Munsterberg

NOTE

The characters on the cover—*shan* (mountain) and *shui* (water), meaning "landscape"—are reproduced from the renowned calligraphy of Kōbō Daishi, Japan's great 9th-century ecclesiast.

The end-paper design reproduces a section from the hemp-cloth landscape in the Shōsō-in, Nara (see page 86).

Contents

LIST OF PLATES.. xi

1. THE SPIRIT OF CHINESE LANDSCAPE PAINTING 3

2. THE BEGINNINGS OF CHINESE LANDSCAPE PAINTING.. 13

3. THE T'ANG PERIOD 19

4. THE FIVE DYNASTIES AND EARLY SUNG PERIODS 29

5. THE NORTHERN SUNG PERIOD 41

6. THE SOUTHERN SUNG PERIOD 49

7. THE YÜAN PERIOD 57

8. THE MING PERIOD 63

CONTENTS

9. THE CH'ING PERIOD 71

10. THE BEGINNINGS OF LANDSCAPE PAINTING IN JAPAN 79

11. THE HEIAN AND KAMAKURA PERIODS 85

12. THE MUROMACHI PERIOD 93

13. THE MOMOYAMA PERIOD 103

14. THE EDO PERIOD 109

15. LANDSCAPE PAINTERS OF THE UKIYO-E SCHOOL 119

NOTES 129

BIBLIOGRAPHY 135

INDEX 139

LIST OF PLATES

Frontispiece. Autumn Landscape, traditionally ascribed to Emperor Hui Tsung, Coll. Konchi-in, Kyoto

1. Ku K'ai-chih: The Nymph of the Lo River (section of scroll), Coll. Freer Gallery of Art, Washington, D.C.

2. Jataka Scene from Cave 110 at Tun Huang, Courtesy L. Warner

3. Sarcophagus with Stories of Filial Piety, Coll. Nelson Gallery of Art, Kansas City

4. Sacrificial House with Scenes of Filial Piety, Coll. Boston Museum of Fine Arts

5. Li Chao-tao (?): Travellers in Mountain Landscape, Coll. National Museum, Peking

6. Li Chao-tao (?): Travellers in Mountain Landscape (detail), Coll. National Museum, Peking

7. After Li Chao-tao: Ch'iu Ch'êng Palace, Coll. Boston Museum of Fine Arts

8. Wang Wei: Wang Ch'uan Scroll (section of scroll), Courtesy Chicago Natural History Museum

9. After Wang Wei: Winter Landscape, Coll. Freer Gallery of Art, Washington, D.C.

10. After Yang Shêng: Misty Landscape, Coll. Metropolitan Museum of Art, New York

11. Anonymous artist: Winter Landscape, Coll. Palace Museum, Peking

12. Ching Hao: View of the K'uan-lu Mountains, Coll. Palace Museum, Peking

13. Li Ch'êng: Travellers Among the Snowy Hills, Coll. Boston Museum of Fine Arts

14. Li Ch'êng: Travellers Among the Snowy Hills (detail), Coll. Boston Museum of Fine Arts

15. Li Ch'êng: Reading the Stele, Coll. Osaka Museum of Art

16. Li Ch'êng (?): Buddhist Temple Amid Clearing Mountain Peaks, Coll. Nelson Gallery of Art, Kansas City

17. Tung Yüan: A Clear Day in the Valley (section of scroll), Coll. Boston Museum of Fine Arts

18. Same

19. Same

20. Tung Yüan: Cave of the Immortals, Coll. Palace Museum, Peking

21. Fan K'uan: Mountain Landscape, Coll. Palace Museum, Peking

22. Fan K'uan: Mountains with Palaces in Snow, Coll. Boston Museum of Fine Arts

23. Anonymous artist: Mountain Landscape, Coll. Nelson Gallery of Art, Kansas City

24. Liao Tomb: Autumn Landscape, Palin, eastern Mongolia

25. Kuo Hsi: An Autumn Day in the Valley of the Yellow River (section of scroll), Coll. Freer Gallery of Art, Washington, D.C.

26. Same

27. Mi Fei: Misty Landscape, Coll. Freer Gallery of Art, Washington, D.C.

28. Mi Fei: Pine Trees and Mountains in Spring, Coll. Palace Museum, Peking

29. Mi Yu-jên: Misty Mountains and River Landscape (section of scroll), Coll. Freer Gallery of Art, Washington, D.C.

30. Same

31. Anonymous artist: Tribute Horse, Coll. Metropolitan Museum of Art, New York

32. Li T'ang: Summer Landscape, Coll. Kōtō-in, Kyoto

33. Li T'ang: Summer Landscape (detail), Coll. Kōtō-in, Kyoto

34. Chao Po-chü: Entry of the First Emperor of the Han Dynasty into Kuan Chung (section of scroll), Coll. Boston Museum of Fine Arts

35. Chao Po-chü: Spring Morning at the Palace of the Han Emperors (section of scroll), Coll. Metropolitan Museum of Art, New York

36. Ma Yüan: Moonlit Night, Coll. Kuroda, Tokyo
37. Ma Yüan: Moonlit Night (detail), Coll. Kuroda, Tokyo
38. Ma Yüan: Bare Willows and Distant Mountains, Coll. Boston Museum of Fine Arts
39. Ma Yüan: The Four Sages of Shang Shan (section of scroll), Coll. Cincinnati Art Museum
40. Hsia Kuei: Summer Landscape, Coll. Iwasaki, Tokyo
41. Hsia Kuei: Mountain and Lake Landscape (section of scroll), Coll. Nelson Gallery of Art, Kansas City
42. Same
43. Same
44. Hsia Kuei: Sailboat in the Rain, Coll. Boston Museum of Fine Arts
45. Ying Yü-chien: Mountain Village in Fog, Coll. Yoshikawa, Tokyo
46. Mu-ch'i: Eight Scenes of Hsiao-Hsiang (section), Coll. Masuda, Tokyo
47. Huang Kung-wang: Fu Ch'un Mountains, Coll. Mr. P'ang Lai-chên, Shanghai
48. Huang Kung-wang (?): Mountain Landscape, Coll. Mr. Mathias Komor, New York
49. Wang Mêng: Landscape Scroll (section of scroll), Coll. Freer Gallery of Art, Washington, D.C.
50. Ni Tsan: Autumn Landscape, Coll. Freer Gallery of Art, Washington, D.C.
51. Hsü Pên: Interminable Rivers and Mountains (section of scroll), Coll. Freer Gallery of Art, Washington, D.C.
52. Kao K'o-kung: Rain in the Mountains, Coll. Detroit Institute of Arts
53. Shên Chou: River Landscape (section of scroll), Coll. Freer Gallery of Art, Washington, D.C.
54. Shên Chou: Poet on a Mountain, Coll. Nelson Gallery of Art, Kansas City
55. Shên Chou: Poet on a Mountain (detail), Coll. Nelson Gallery of Art, Kansas City
56. Tai Chin: Autumn River Landscape with Fishing Boats (section of

scroll), Coll. Freer Gallery of Art, Washington, D.C.

57. Same

58. Tai Chin: River Landscape (section of scroll), Coll. Freer Gallery of Art, Washington, D.C.

59. Same

60. Wên Chêng-ming: Landscape Scroll (section of scroll), Coll. Freer Gallery of Art, Washington, D.C.

61. T'ang Yin: Mountain Landscape (section of scroll), Coll. Freer Gallery of Art, Washington, D.C.

62. Ch'iu Ying: Garden Feast, Coll. Chion-in, Kyoto

63. Wang Hui: Mount Fu Ch'un (section of scroll), Coll. Freer Gallery of Art, Washington, D.C.

64. Same

65. Shih-t'ao: Mountain Landscape, Coll. Nü Wa Chai, China

66. Pa-ta Shan-jên: Rocks and Fish, Private Collection, New York

67. Yüan Chiang: Carts on a Winding Mountain Road, Coll. Nelson Gallery of Art, Kansas City

68. Anonymous artist: Sages in a Landscape (section of scroll), Coll. Freer Gallery of Art, Washington, D.C.

69. Wang Cheng-kuo: Landscape Scroll, Coll. Mr. Mathias Komor, New York

70. Wang Chi-ch'üan: Rocks and Water, Coll. the artist, New York

71. Jataka Scene from Tamamushi Shrine, Coll. Hōryū-ji, Nara

72. Kako Genzai Inga Kyō (section of scroll), Coll. Jōhōrendai-ji, Kyoto

73. Plectrum Guard of Biwa, Coll. Shōsō-in, Nara

74. Hemp Cloth with Landscape (detail), Coll. Shōsō-in, Nara

75. Senzui Byōbu, Coll. Tō-ji, Kyoto

76. Shigisan Engi Scroll (section), Coll. Chōgosonshi-ji, Nara

77. Senzui Byōbu, (section), Coll. Jingo-ji, Kyoto

78. Nachi Waterfall, Coll. Nezu Museum, Tokyo

79. Shūbun: Landscape Scroll, Coll. Fujiwara, Tokyo

80. Sesshū: Landscape Scroll (section), Coll. Mōri, Tokyo

81. Sesshū: Landscape, Coll. National Museum, Tokyo

82. Sōami: Landscape, Coll. Daisen-in, Daitoku-ji, Kyoto

83. Motonobu: Priest Ling-yün Viewing Peach Blossoms, Coll. National Museum, Tokyo
84. Sesson: Landscape, Coll. Nomura, Kyoto
85. Kano Eitoku: Hawk on Pine Screen, Coll. University of Arts, Tokyo
86. Unknown artist: Uji Bridge Screen, Private Collection, Tokyo
87. Kaihō Yūshō: Screen with Fishing Nets, Coll. National Museum, Tokyo
88. Hasegawa Tōhaku: Screen with Pines, Coll. National Museum, Tokyo
89. Kano Naonobu: Landscape Screen, Coll. National Museum, Tokyo
90. Sōtatsu: Genji Monogatari Screen (detail), Coll. Seikadō Bunko, Tokyo
91. Ogata Kōrin: Plum Tree Screen, Coll. Tsugaru, Tokyo
92. Ikeno Taiga: Convenience of Farming, Coll. Kawabata, Kamakura
93. Gyokudō: Mountain Landscape, Coll. Yamaguchi, Kyoto
94. Maruyama Ōkyo: Hozu River Screen (detail), Coll. Nishimura, Kyoto
95. Goshun: Snow Scene Screen (section), Coll. National Museum, Tokyo
96. Shiba Kōkan: Shinobazu-no-Ike, Coll. National Museum, Tokyo
97. Hokusai: Fuji in Clear Weather, Coll. National Museum, Tokyo
98. Hokusai: Fujimihara, Coll. National Museum, Tokyo
99. Hiroshige: Shower at Atake Bridge, Coll. National Museum, Tokyo
100. Hiroshige: Fuji at Yui, Coll. National Museum, Tokyo
101. Hiroshige: Snow at Kameyama, Coll. National Museum, Tokyo

The Landscape Painting
of
CHINA

NOTE

The Japanese suffix *-in* signifies an important institution (usually Buddhist), and the suffixes *-ji* and *-dera* signify Buddhist temples.

1
The Spirit of Chinese
Landscape Painting

LONG before the emergence of Chinese landscape painting, the Chinese venerated the forces of nature. The earliest written documents, the inscribed oracle bones from the ancient Shang capital of An-yang, refer to the spirits of the mountains and rivers, to the deities of heaven and earth, and to the directions. China's oldest poetry, the Shih Ching, or Book of Song, dating from around 1000 B.C., not only shows a keen sense of the loveliness of nature but also relates man to it, as in the following verse:

> Gorgeous in their beauty
> Are the flowers of the cherry:
> Are they not magnificent in their dignity
> The carriages of the royal bride.

Another song uses these images:

> How the cloth-plant spreads
> Across the midst of the valley!
> Thick grow its leaves,
> The oriole in its flight
> Perches on that copse,
> Its song is full of longing.[1]

Not only the priests and poets of ancient China but also the great philosophers of the Chou period, like Confucius and Lao-tzu, conceived of man as governed by the forces of heaven and earth. Confucius in one place says: "The wise find pleasure in water, the virtuous find pleasure in hills."[2] And Lao-tzu writes:

> Heaven is eternal, the Earth is everlasting.
> How come they to be so? It is because they do not
>   foster their own lives,
> That is why they live so long.
> Therefore the Sage
> Puts himself in the background; but is also to the fore.
> Remains outside; but is always there.
> Is it not just because he does not strive for personal ends
> That all his personal ends are fulfilled.[3]

Here in the words of the ancient sages one finds the very spirit which, centuries later, was to be perfectly expressed in the art of the landscape. In China alone, landscape painting has religious as well as philosophical significance, and for over a thousand years it was regarded as the most important subject matter for the artist. Chinese landscape painting in consequence is one of the great manifestations of the human spirit as well as the most remarkable creation of the Chinese artistic genius. The term "landscape," or *shan shui* in Chinese, combines the same two concepts which Confucius mentioned, for it consists of the characters for mountain and water. This in itself is deeply meaningful, suggesting as it does the very elements which were considered the most important in rendering nature. The sacred mountains of China have been worshipped from time immemorial, and the Five Sacred Peaks form one of the *Shih-erh Chang,* or Twelve Ancient Ornaments. Water also was of prime significance to an agricultural people like the Chinese, and it was worshipped in the form of rivers, clouds, mist, and rain, and symbolized by the dragon, one of the most ancient and popular of Chinese sacred animals. Lao-tzu, in yet another passage of his famous Tao Tê Ching, uses water as an illustration of the Supreme, the Tao, when he says:

The highest good is like that of water. The goodness of water is that it benefits the ten thousand creatures, yet it does not scramble but is content with the places that all men disdain. It is this that makes water so near to the Way.[4]

It is no pure chance that Taoist thought exerted such a profound influence on the landscape painters of China, for here was a philosophy which taught man to lose himself in the vastness of nature so that he might find himself, to identify his soul with the Spirit which pervades the cosmos, the Ultimate Essense, the Tao, in order to gain insight into the nature of reality. Taoist mysticism and the closely related Ch'an, or Zen, Buddhism, dedicated to a very similar type of mystic experience, were the primary intellectual and spiritual forces leading to the great florescence of landscape painting during the Sung period. Precisely at that time the merger of these tendencies took place, and it was then that they enjoyed their greatest popularity among the people of education and culture.[5]

Besides mountains and rivers, trees constituted a third element considered indispensable to any true landscape. It is perhaps in representing these that the Chinese artist showed his greatest insight into the structure of nature, for while Western artists were usually content with an exterior likeness, the Chinese painter wished to portray the very essence of the tree. After absorbing their shape and manner of growth and trying to identify himself with their spirit, he was able to give his trees an individuality and expressiveness which no Western artist has achieved. To the painters of China, the tree (or the mountain or the rock) was as important as man himself, and thus it was rendered with equal if not greater care and with so much feeling that its very life is revealed, and even a Westerner, no matter how different his view of nature, will find that he looks at trees with a new understanding after studying Chinese landscape paintings.

Among the trees painted, the pine is the most beloved, for the pine, with its "straight-stemmed trunk and gnarled and twisted branches, typifies the scholar-official who may be shaken by the wind of calumny and misfortune, but remains erect and steadfast, his character rooted in the unchanging principles of Confucian virtue."[6] A great variety of pines and other evergreens are found in the landscapes, represented singly or in groups, silhouetted against the sky or seen on mountains. Next to the pine in popularity is the bamboo. In fact, a whole branch of Chinese painting is devoted to this beautiful tree. Like the pine, the bamboo has a symbolic meaning for the

5

Chinese, standing "for lasting friendship and hardy age, but especially for *chü-jên* (a gentleman), for it bows to the storm but rises again when the storm has abated."[7] These two trees, together with the blossoming plum tree, which was thought of as a harbinger of spring, are referred to as the three friends of the cold season. Other trees often represented are the willow, which is especially popular in Sung painting, the arborvitae, catalpa, oak, elm, mulberry, and a generalized type of tree which cannot be identified with any particular genus.

Though mountains, water, and trees are the main elements of landscape painting, this does not mean that the artist restricted himself to these. Rocks also played an important role, and some of the early Ch'ing painters, such as Shih-t'ao, were famous for their wonderful rendering of picturesque stones. Besides these, many different kinds of grass, moss, bushes, and flowers are represented, and romantic waterfalls and gorges were much admired, emphasizing as they do the grandeur and wildness of nature. In the midst of these natural phenomena, the artist, especially in the Sung and Ming periods, placed a tiny hut and a sage or two lost in rapt admiration of the vastness and beauty of the landscape. The onlooker, in turn, was supposed to identify himself with the tiny figure, letting his spirit dwell in the imaginary scene so that he too might find peace in the contemplation of nature.

The mentality of the gentleman-scholar who devoted himself to landscape painting is perhaps best expressed in Kuo Hsi's famous "Essay on Landscape Painting," which, although written in the eleventh century, served as a model and source of inspiration for all subsequent Chinese landscape painters. In it the author, himself a famous painter, says:

Why does a virtuous man take delight in landscape? It is for these reasons: that in a rustic retreat he may nourish nature; that amid the carefree play of streams and rocks, he may take delight; that he may constantly meet in the country fishermen, woodcutters, and hermits, and see the soaring cranes, and hear the crying of the monkeys. The din of the dusty world and the locked-in-ness of human habitations are what human nature habitually abhors; while, on the contrary, haze, mist, and the haunting spirits of the mountains are what human nature seeks, and yet can rarely find. When, however, in the heyday of great peace and prosperity, the minds, both of man's sovereign and of his parents, are full of high expectations of his services, should he still stand aloof, neglecting the responsibilities of honor and righteousness? In face of such duties the benevolent man cannot seclude himself and shun the world.

6

He cannot hope to equal in spirit virtuous hermits such as Chi Tzu and Yin Hsü-yu or share the name of Hsia Huang-kung and Ch'i Li-chi.[8]

Since in doing his duty to society the lover of landscapes is cut off from the joys of nature, it is to the painting of landscapes that he must turn in order to participate, in spirit at least, in these delights, and Kuo Hsi goes on to say:

Having no access to the landscape, the lover of forest and stream, the friend of mist and haze, enjoys them only in his dreams. How delightful then to have a landscape painted by a skilled hand! Without leaving the room, at once, he finds himself among the streams and ravines; the cries of the birds and monkeys are faintly audible to his senses; light on the hills and reflections on the water, glittering, dazzle his eyes. Does not such a scene satisfy his mind and captivate his heart? That is why the world values the true significance of the painting of mountains. If this is not recognized, and the landscapes are roughly and carelessly approached, then is it not like spoiling a magnificent view and polluting the pure wind?[9]

Thus the onlooker, reverently unrolling a painting, was invited to identify himself with the tiny figures wandering about the valleys, standing at the water's edge, or contemplating the scenery. Kuo Hsi, discussing the different types of landscape, talks of those in which one can travel, those which can be gazed upon, those in which one can ramble, and finally, those in which one can dwell, stressing that it is the last two which are most praiseworthy. Few, he says, will ever achieve this effect, but these beautiful works arouse in the superior man the yearning for forest and stream. This emphasis on the landscape itself is peculiar to Chinese painting: in most Western art, the landscape is merely a backdrop for human activity, while here the reverse is the case, and man is subordinate to the immensity of nature.

In selecting a particular motif, the artist often drew upon traditional subjects, especially scenes which had been celebrated by the poets of the past, such as Li Po or Tu Fu. There is a Chinese saying that poetry is a picture without form and painting a poem with form, and a few lines from a lyric often served both as inspiration and subject matter. Kuo Hsi, discussing poetry, wrote: "The beautiful lines give full expression to the inmost thoughts of men's souls, and describe vividly the scenery before men's eyes."[10] One of the most popular subjects was the group of eight views of the Hsiao and Hsiang Rivers, each of which represents a scene from the shores of Lake

7

Tung-t'ing that Li Po had celebrated in the following famous poem:

On the Tung-t'ing Lake

Westward from Tung-t'ing the Chu River branches out,
While the lake fades into the cloudless sky of the south.
The sun gone down, the autumn twilight steals far over Chang-sha;
I wonder where sleep the lost queens of Hsiang of old.[11]

The very titles of these views are deeply suggestive of the spirit of this kind of landscape painting: The Evening Bell from a Distant Temple, Sunset Glow over a Fishing Village, Fine Weather after Storm at a Lonely Mountain Town, Homeward-Bound Boats off a Distant Coast, The Autumn Moon over Lake Tung-t'ing, Wild Geese Alighting on a Sandy Plain, Night Rain on the Rivers Hsiao and Hsiang, and Evening Snow on the Hills.

Other paintings show the valley of the Yellow River, a fisherman in a boat, a hermit in the mountains, a sage gazing at the moon or visiting a friend in his retreat, mist over the mountain tops, and many similar scenes. The overwhelming aspect of nature, especially of mountains, and the minuteness of man contemplating this majesty are the ever-recurring subjects of Chinese painting. In depicting such scenes, the artist was taught that he must first of all identify himself with the landscape and become one with the Tao which pervades all of nature, for only then could he begin to do justice to his theme. He was not concerned with that outward appearance of nature which absorbed the French Impressionists, but rather with its innermost spirit. Thus, he concentrated on the essentials, for only in so doing would he be able to present the soul of the cosmos. We are told over and over again how the great painters of China would spend months and even years wandering through mountain landscapes, immersing themselves in the forms of nature until they had discovered their true being; and then, and only then, would they take up their brushes and record their impressions. Preparatory sketches of the type common in our civilization are almost unknown in Chinese art, and painting directly from the scene itself was very rare, for the artist, after having achieved a mystical identification with the spirit of nature, recreated the vision from within himself.

Although the landscapes are often identified by name, and certain famous motifs are done again and again, this does not mean that these paintings are

8

to be thought of as realistic versions of particular scenes, painted the way a Courbet might have painted an actual place, but rather that these traditionally admired sights were considered ideal landscapes. These scrolls were the expression of a cultural ideal which during the Sung period and after dominated the artistic output of the Chinese painter-scholars. During later periods, such as the Ming and Ch'ing dynasties, artists often derived their inspiration not from an actual scene but from a celebrated scroll by some painter whom they particularly admired, usually one of the great masters of the T'ang, Sung, or Yüan periods. This is not to say that these works were outright copies but rather that they were painted in the spirit of the artist who had inspired the work, so that the earlier painter became a kind of godfather to the later one. This, in a way, assured the continuity of the great artistic tradition of China, but at the same time it often had a stultifying effect upon the output of later periods, when a dead academicism replaced the vital artistic spirit which had prevailed in earlier times. This attitude also creates particular problems for the historian and the connoisseur of Chinese painting, since it becomes next to impossible to determine with certainty which scrolls are by the artists to whom they are ascribed and which are no more than copies of originals or works inspired by some famous masterpiece of one of the great painters of the past.

The landscapes represented were shown in a variety of moods depending upon the time of day, the weather, and the season of the year. There were morning or evening views, rainy or sunny scenes, tempestuous or tranquil ones, each represented in its own peculiar manner. As Kuo Hsi had said:

The spring mountain is wrapped in an unbroken stretch of dreamy haze and mist, and men are joyful; the summer mountain is rich with shady foliage, and men are peaceful; the autumn mountain is serene and calm, with leaves falling, and men are solemn; the winter mountain is heavy with storm clouds and withdrawn, and men are forlorn.

The sight of such pictured mountains arouses in men exactly corresponding moods. It is as if he were actually in those mountains. They exist as if they were real, not painted. The blue haze and white path arouse a longing to walk there; the sunset on a quiet stream arouses a longing to gaze upon it; the sight of hermits and ascetics arouses a longing to dwell with them; the rocks and streams arouse a longing to saunter among them ... the meaning of these pictures is wonderful.[12]

9

In painting these scenes the artist was not expected to give a life-like and detailed view, but rather a general impression which would convey to the onlooker a feeling of the scene as a whole. Too many intricacies would only interfere with his vision, for, as Kuo Hsi wrote: "When the artist succeeds in reproducing this general tone and not a group of disjointed forms, then clouds and atmosphere seem to come to life." Perhaps this ability to bring many details together into a unified and expressive whole, alive with the very spirit of nature, is the quality which distinguishes the great masters of Chinese painting from their many imitators and followers. These lesser men might be able, technically, to render every detail as the painter's manual had prescribed it, but they could not fuse these elements into a meaningful whole, and the result is an art both academic and eclectic, without any of the mysterious power which so pervades the masterpieces of Chinese painting. It is this that Hsieh Ho, the great fifth-century critic, had in mind when he made his first principle of painting the rendering of the "spirit-resonance and life-movement," or *ch'i-yün shêng-tung* in Chinese,[13] a principle that lies at the very core of the Chinese conception of art. If the painter possessed this, he was, through inspiration, able to grasp the mysterious quality of nature, while if he lacked it, then the greatest technical virtuosity was as nothing. In a critic like Hsieh Ho, the dual nature of the Chinese mind is clearly revealed, and, as in Confucius and Lao-tzu, the rational and the emotional, the practical and the mystic both find expression. Thus Hsieh Ho in his six canons lists five which are basically technical. The second principle is the "bone manner," or structural use of the brush, while in the third he tells the artist to conform with the objects to obtain their likeness. The fourth says that the colors should be applied according to the species; the fifth deals with composition, which Siren has translated as "plan and design, place and position"; and the sixth says to transmit models by drawing.[14] However, he begins with the first and most important, the *ch'i-yün shêng-tung,* which is as elusive and profound as the writings of Lao-tzu. Yet both are essential to Chinese art, and they must exist side by side, for in any really great work technique and inspiration are inseparably united. In the last analysis, even the greatest inspiration is worthless if the artist does not have the skill to give expression to it, and on the other hand, even the greatest

10

technical ability is of little value when the artist lacks inspiration.

A unique feature of Chinese painting which distinguishes it from that of the West is its close relationship to calligraphy, a relationship that has certainly existed since Han times, that is, for at least two thousand years. The great artists of China were often as highly esteemed as calligraphers as they were as painters, and the skillful and artistic use of the brush played an essential role in the training of every person of education. Another difference between China and the West is that the Chinese artists were, more likely than not, gentlemen-painters rather than professionals, many being officials, statesmen, or even generals and emperors. This cultural ideal of the gentleman-painter, who is an amateur in the best sense of the word, is aptly described in the introduction to the catalogue of the collection of the most famous of all the gentlemen-painters, the Emperor Hui Tsung of the Sung dynasty, an artist of considerable talent who assembled one of the most magnificent collections of Chinese painting ever known. In the catalogue he says that the famous landscape painters from the T'ang to the Sung period were by and large not professionals but high officials and scholars who carried their vision of hills and valleys in their hearts, were in love with springs and stones, and had a great weakness for mists and clouds. He ends by saying that landscape paintings cannot be sold in the street, for they do not correspond to the taste of the common people.[15]

2

The Beginnings of Chinese
Landscape Painting

THE earliest landscapes in Chinese art are found in the Han period (202 B.C.—220 A.D.) some two thousand years ago. At that time mountains, clouds, trees, and buildings first appeared in relief carvings, textile designs, mirror backs, and inlaid metal objects, but the elements of nature were rendered in a highly symbolic and abstract way. Although similar forms must also have appeared in the paintings of the period, no examples of such works have survived, and our knowledge, at best, is fragmentary. However, the evidence clearly suggests that nothing but the most stylized and primitive kind of landscape setting appeared in these early examples of landscape painting. The main elements were no doubt highly simplified, with very geometric trees and mountains rendered so abstractly that they would hardly have been recognizable. The reason for this was not so much a lack of skill on the part of the artists, since Han painters were in many ways highly competent, even sophisticated craftsmen; it was rather that they concentrated more on figure painting, devoting their major effort to the portrayal of scenes from myths, legends, history, and filial piety, and hence were little interested in landscape painting as such.

It was not until the following era, the Six Dynasties period (265—589), that landscape painting as such began. This development, according to Chinese tradition, is associated with one of the most celebrated of all Chinese artists, the great painter, calligrapher, and wit Ku K'ai-chih, who worked during the second half of the fourth century in the Southern capital at Nanking. Although he too regarded figure painting and portraiture as the most significant class of painting, he was nevertheless the first to accord landscape its proper place. A description of a real or imaginary landscape painted by Ku K'ai-chih has been preserved in an essay entitled *Hua Yün-t'ai Shan Chi,* or "How to Paint the Cloud-Terrace Mountain."[16] How far this still was from naturalism is best seen by the fact that it was a Taoist landscape with peach trees of long life. In painting it, the artist said that he would make "purple rocks looking something like solid clouds, five or six of them astride the hill. And ascending between them there should be shapes that writhe and coil like dragons."[17] Certainly the kind of landscape suggested in the essay must have been primitive in the extreme. The famous T'ang critic Chang Yen-yüan, writing in 847, five hundred years later, when presumably the originals by Ku K'ai-chih were still extant, says:

There are some famous pictures handed down from the Wei and Chin dynasties, and I have had occasion to see them. The landscapes are filled with crowded peaks, their effect is like that of filigree ornaments or horn combs. Sometimes the water does not seem to flow, sometimes the figures are larger than the mountains. The views are generally enclosed by trees and stones which stand in a circle on the ground. They look like rows of lifted arms with outspread fingers.[18]

No originals by Ku K'ai-chih have been preserved, but fortunately two excellent copies have survived. The first is the famous "Admonitions of the Imperial Preceptress" scroll, formerly in the imperial collection in Peking and now in the British Museum in London, which is believed to be a T'ang copy of a famous Ku K'ai-chih painting. One of the scenes shows a huntsman with a bow kneeling at the foot of a mountain and aiming at some birds in the distance.[19] The relation between the figures and the mountain, both in relative size and in space, is wholly unnaturalistic, although the mountain itself, with its rising peaks, deep valleys, and dropping cliffs, is rendered very convincingly.

Another copy after Ku K'ai-chih, which is far better preserved and, although of later date, closer in style to what an original of the fourth century must have looked like, is in the Freer Gallery of Art in Washington. It comes from the Sung period, probably the twelfth century, and represents the tale of the nymph of the Lo River *(Plate 1)*. A continuous scroll in which figures are seen in a landscape, the painting illustrates very clearly the primitive kind of landscape typical of the period. In the detail shown, the figures are too large in relation to the landscape which, as in the work of Italian Primitives like Giotto, is little more than a setting for human activity. The mountains in the left foreground are so stylized that at first glance one hardly recognizes them, and the trees, climbing up the slopes and standing in front, have no consistent relationship in size, either among themselves or to the mountains. One tree soars high above the tallest peak; another, a willow, is the same size as the mountains; and the rest are as small as a single branch of the largest tree. In the middle foreground the trees are much shorter than those standing above in back, and the ship at the right is too small in relation to the figures. Each part—the mountains, the figures, the ship—is almost a unit in itself, and neither in space nor in perspective has the painter succeeded in fusing the parts into a whole. The treatment of the landscape is still highly decorative and corresponds very closely to Chang Yen-yüan's description. It is clear that Ku K'ai-chih has attempted to show figures in a natural setting, relating them to the space and to the scenery, but it is equally clear that his ability to render the setting convincingly is still inadequate, and the result, though charming in an archaic sort of way, is not successful as a landscape.

A somewhat younger contemporary of Ku K'ai-chih who lived on into the fifth century was Tsung Ping (375—443), of whom unfortunately no paintings have been preserved. We are told, however, that he was famous for his landscape paintings and that he roamed about the mountain wilderness, playing his lute and enjoying the beauty and grandeur of nature. When he grew old he painted some of his favorite scenes on the walls of his house and lamented the fact that he could no longer wander in the mountains. He wrote a brief essay entitled *Shan Shui Sü,* or "Introduction to Landscape Painting," which shows a sentiment closely allied to that of the great

15

landscape painters of later periods and is clearly Taoist in inspiration. In it he says:

Landscapes exist in material substance and soar into the realm of the spirit.... Taoists travelled among the mountains.... Such sojourning has often been called finding pleasure in mountains and water by the virtuous and wise. The virtuous man follows the Way (Tao) by spiritual insight, the wise man takes this same approach. But the lovers of landscapes are led into the Way by a sense of form. The virtuous man also takes pleasure in this. Then, are not the pleasures of the virtuous and wise similar to those of the lovers of landscape?[20]

No doubt landscape painting itself underwent considerable development during the fifth century, but unfortunately no authentic scrolls from this period have survived. The only original which may be traced back to the fifth century is a wall painting in cave Number 110 at the famous Buddhist site of Tun Huang at the westernmost frontier of China. Here, in a Jataka scene depicting a Buddhist legend, there is a mountain landscape which perhaps gives some idea of what the landscape painting of this period may have been like (Plate 2). However, it must be said that Tun Huang was far off in the provinces and that these works, although invaluable for us today, were only a crude reflection of the style current at the imperial court and in the other cultural centers. It must have taken a generation or more for the latest artistic developments to reach this outpost, and it may be assumed that the painters active here were provincial artisans who cannot be compared with such great masters as Ku K'ai-chih and Tsung Ping. However, even when this has been taken into account, one must conclude that little real progress had been made during the century. In the detail shown, the treatment of the landscape is far more decorative than that of the "Nymph of the Lo River" scroll. While Ku K'ai-chih varied the arrangement of his trees and mountains, showing them in groups or singly in silhouettes and placing some parallel to the bottom of the painting and others diagonally, the artist at Tun Huang made a pattern of the natural elements. The mountains, each with one slope straight and the other jagged, are set side by side in groups which are rhythmically repeated and so stylized that one cannot be sure they are mountains. In considering this work, however, it must be borne in mind that the landscape is only the setting for

16

a Buddhist wall painting; although none have survived, there must have been landscape scrolls painted during the period which showed a more advanced style.

With the sixth century, developments reached a climax which led to the establishment of true landscape painting. Again we are greatly handicapped by the lack of authentic paintings, but other artistic monuments such as engraved stone slabs give a good idea of the style which prevailed during the century. The finest and most famous of these is the stone sarcophagus in the Nelson Gallery of Art in Kansas City, whose incised side panels represent stories of filial piety *(Plate 3)*. Now, for the first time, the figures are rendered in proper proportion to the setting, and they move among the trees and rocks in a natural and convincing way. There is also a real feeling of space, with the eye of the observer being led into the distance. The free-flowing line is employed with both skill and elegance, pointing up the picturesque shapes of the trees and rock formations. However, even here the artist's main emphasis is upon the Confucian story, and the landscape is, in the last analysis, merely a setting for the figures shown. This is certainly typical of that age, though it may be assumed that some pure landscapes were painted at the time, even if Buddhist and Confucian scenes with landscape settings were the more popular subject.

The other work which reflects the style of the age convincingly is a sacrificial stone house in the Museum of Fine Arts in Boston *(Plate 4)*. It is dated 529 and is similar in style to the Kansas City sarcophagus. Again, the scenes depict episodes of filial piety, but the emphasis is more on the interior setting than the outdoor landscape. However, the manner of representation is very like that of the sarcophagus in the Nelson Gallery, with delicately incised lines suggesting the contours of the objects. In the immediate foreground, rocks, grasses, trees, and undulating earth are rendered with the greatest economy and with the inspired and dynamic use of line so typical of the period. Above, figures in the building are engaged in various activities, and in the background, a variety of trees loom over the tiled roofs. The slanting parallel lines in the right side of the building indicate the artist's attempt to give perspective, thus showing that the rendering of space in depth is a problem with which he is consciously struggling. The quality of the execution here, as well as in the sarcophagus, is very fine, and it may be assumed that these works reflect the most advanced artistic style. It would thus appear that the sixth century already knew landscape painting as a distinct genre, but that the nature of the landscape was still stylized and decorative.

3

The T'ang Period

NOT until the T'ang period (618—907) did landscape painting evolve into a separate and major genre of Chinese painting. This age, in fact, was looked upon by later critics as a golden age, during which some of the greatest artistic figures were active. How much of this estimate was based upon actual knowledge of their works and how much is the characteristically Chinese veneration of all that is ancient and traditional is hard to tell, but even the famous Sung scholar Su Tung-po complained in 1085 that only one or two original scrolls by Wu Tao-tzu could be found. Today the situation is even worse, and it is doubtful if there is more than one true T'ang landscape in existence. This state of affairs is very similar to that in Greek art, where we have numerous literary references to the famous sculptors of the Golden Age but few if any originals which can be attributed to them with certainty, since all the surviving works are either Roman copies or minor works by anonymous artists.

The first of the four great artistic figures who dominated this period was Li Ssu-hsün, known as General Li, who was probably born around 650 and died in 716. His fame was no doubt due just as much to his high social position and official rank as to his artistic accomplishments, for he was a descendant of the founder of the T'ang dynasty. Critics such as the celebrated Sung painter Mi Fei and the Ming scholar Tung Ch'i-ch'ang considered his work rather dry and poor, and his painting was no doubt somewhat academic, belonging to that tradition which emphasized meticulous detail and bright colors, a style referred to by the Chinese as *kung pi*. He was, however, greatly admired by the T'ang critics as, for example, the ninth-century scholar Chu Ching-hsüan, who, in *The Famous Painters of the T'ang Dynasty,* written in 840, refers to his style as lofty and original and says that his landscapes were supremely excellent,[21] adding that the Emperor Ming Huang considered them the best of the period. According to these accounts, Li Ssu-hsün painted elaborate landscapes with palaces, pavilions, bridges, and terraces all brightly colored in blues and greens and reds and whites and done with a wealth of detail in a meticulous and refined manner. Unfortunately, none of his works have survived, and those connected with his name are at best very late reflections of his style.

If Li Ssu-hsün, at the end of the seventh century, had prepared the way for the florescence of Chinese landscape painting during the eighth, it was Wu Tao-tzu (*ca.* 680—760) who was the dominating artistic personality of this period. Again we are completely dependent upon literary evidence, because among the paintings and rubbings which today are associated with his name none are landscapes. His fame probably rested for the most part upon his Buddhist and figure paintings, but even here the few extant works ascribed to him are nothing but weak reflections of what his style must have been. According to tradition, his contribution to the development of landscape painting was considerable, and such a famous T'ang critic as Chang Yen-yüan, writing only a century after the death of the artist, said that he was one of the pioneers in the evolution of T'ang landscape painting. He wrote that, although the old manner gradually changed, the painters still shaped stones like dripping ice crystals and drew every fiber and carved every leaf of the trees. Of all of the artists only Wu Tao-tzu's brushwork was inspired by heaven, and Chang Yen-yüan says that Wu Tao-tzu, working in a new and more plastic style, often painted strange rocks and broken river banks on temple walls. He adds that, when Wu Tao-tzu went to Shu, he created landscapes which transformed the art of landscape painting.[22] Today we have little to go on in trying to reconstruct the type of landscape Wu Tao-tzu painted, but since the Chinese critics always stress the boldness and

20

power of his brush stroke, and a famous story told by the ninth-century critic Chu Ching-hsüan relates that he completed a panorama of over three hundred *li* in a single day, we may assume that it was a loose, free type of painting, a style very different from that of Li Ssu-hsün. Another story is that, when the emperor asked to see his sketches, Wu replied that he had none, for he had set them down in his heart. It is said that the Emperor Ming Huang also commissioned General Li to do a painting for the same building and that it took him several months to complete it. The emperor's comment was: "Li Ssu-hsün's achievement of many months, Wu Tao-tzu's of a single day...both are excellent in the extreme."[23] Although this story must be legendary, since Li was no longer alive at the time, it nevertheless illustrates the style of painting associated with these two artists during the T'ang period, when their works were no doubt readily available to the scholars and connoisseurs. Of course wall paintings such as these would deteriorate rapidly, and today we have no idea of what they looked like.

Although Li Ssu-hsün was dead at this time, his work was being carried on by his son, Li Chao-tao (*ca.* 670—730), who was a painter famous in his own right. Tradition has it that his works were very similar to those of his father, except that they lacked the elder Li's creative power and strength of brush stroke. Unfortunately, we are not in a position to compare their work, but it would seem likely that the younger Li, coming at a later time, would have shown a somewhat more advanced manner of painting landscapes. His works were apparently still quite numerous during the ninth century, and even today there are at least two paintings to which Li Chao-tao's name has become attached and which, even if not by his own hand, certainly reflect his style. The first, a small colored landscape painted on silk, which is in the Peking National Museum, represents travellers in a mountain landscape *(Plate 5).* This may well be an eighth-century original, for the closeness of its style to that of similar scenes painted on musical instruments in the Shōsō-in in Nara is striking. The manner of painting is extremely meticulous, and the many details are executed with sharply defined linear accents. The bright colors are typical of this type of T'ang painting, which is known as *ch'ing lü shan shui,* since the dominant colors are always blue and green, though in this painting there are greys and red as well.

21

The scene represented in the detail *(Plate 6)* shows a mountainous landscape with steep cliffs and valleys through which a group of men on horseback are travelling, accompanied by camels with heavy burdens. Decorative, picturesquely-shaped trees are scattered through the valley, while along the ridges and peaks groups of tiny trees are set like combs. Highly stylized clouds swirl around the mountain tops, sometimes isolating them like islands and sometimes hanging above the peaks in the distance. Riders emerge from the right background and move down towards the front to a bridge leading over a stream, while in the center some travellers are resting, others are unloading the beasts of burden, and unsaddled horses are lying beneath the trees. At the left, still another group is riding up a winding path, and tiny figures appear far above on the mountain. All this is shown with a wealth of minute and beautiful detail, but the painting lacks the kind of unity and grandeur which the great landscapes of the Sung period possess. It is also interesting to note that this is by no means a pure landscape in the Sung sense, for the figures, far from being subordinate to the majesty of nature, are still the center of interest, while the mountains are to a certain extent a setting for the travellers. Although a long step has been taken from the sixth century, when the figures were still completely dominant, this is not landscape painting for its own sake but rather a transitional work where the figures and the landscape coexist as equals.

Another painting that has been traditionally associated with Li Chao-tao because of a label which was later attached to it is a landscape scroll in the Boston Museum of Fine Arts *(Plate 7)*. The subject, the Ch'iu Ch'êng Palace, a summer abode of the T'ang emperors, is typical of an age characterized by splendor and material wealth. It seems unlikely that this work was actually by Li Chao-tao himself, but it may well be by a Sung artist copying one of his designs or painting in his manner. The whole problem of attribution in Chinese painting is an extremely complex one, and even the most eminent connoisseurs will differ fundamentally over questions of attribution. The reason is that, not only did the Chinese throughout their history assiduously copy the old masters, often with remarkable skill, but when doing so they also copied the signature, seals, and colophons. Likewise, they painted in the manner of an old master, not with any intention of deceiving but rather to show their veneration for the great artist in whose style they were working. Finally, in modern times, there are copies which are outright forgeries of older paintings. These, which sometimes are of very good quality, include all the proper inscriptions and seals mentioned in the literature, so that it is often difficult to detect them, especially if the original has been lost or is not readily available for comparison. The result is that dozens of works may bear the name of a celebrated artist without there being much likelihood that a single one so inscribed is actually by the artist whose seal and signature appear on the painting. And since in the Sung period critics were already lamenting the fact that most of the T'ang works they saw were later copies, it is clear that we have at best more or less accurate later versions of the works of the great T'ang masters which may or may not give us a notion of what the work of a given artist was like.

The Boston painting, at least in its subject matter and execution, is undoubtedly close to the work of both the elder and the younger Li, for we are told that they often painted the splendid palaces of the age in an elaborate, brightly colored manner. Today these colors are unfortunately faded, but even so the red, blue, green, and grey still create a vivid effect. Here again, as in the Peking landscape, the world of nature is subordinate to man's activity, and the emphasis is placed not so much upon the trees and the mountains, beautifully as they are rendered, but upon the palace itself and the people. There is a multitude of descriptive detail, of doorways, courts, stairs, tiles, all drawn with exquisite care, so that the magnificence of the palace architecture may be fully appreciated. However, the more fluent and natural rendition of the willow trees in the foreground and the simple, rather abstract treatment of the mountain tops, combined with the greater awareness of space and atmosphere, suggest that this is the work of a later date, even if the general spirit is close to that of the T'ang period.

There is another painting often attributed to Li Chao-tao, one representing a similar subject—the Lo-yang Mansion—which, like the "Mountain Landscape with Travellers," is owned by the Chinese government and used to be in the Palace Museum in Peking.[24] The motif is close to the spirit of the T'ang period as well as to the kind of subject then popular, but the execution

23

is very different from that which we would expect in a genuine T'ang painting. The brush strokes are hard and dry, the whole over-elaborate, suggesting a later copy made by a minor artist who may have seen an original but certainly did not have the talent to reproduce it. Furthermore, the rendering of the atmosphere, especially the mist covering the water and the mountains, proves conclusively that it is the work of a later age.

There are in the collection of the Peking Palace Museum two other paintings by an anonymous artist, one depicting Tu Fu's poem entitled *Li Jen Hsing* and the other called "Snowing in Shen Lin Garden,"[25] both of which in style and subject matter are close to the works discussed above. They are rather poor in quality but for that reason probably closer to the originals than they would have been if the artist who painted them had had a stronger artistic personality. They are no doubt Sung works, though they are done in a very archaic style which, with its elaborate treatment of the architecture and detailed rendition of the mountains, is quite in keeping with what we would expect from the T'ang period. Finally, there is a painting in the collection of Professor Ogawa in Kyoto which is traditionally attributed to Li Chao-tao,[26] a long narrative scroll showing a typical T'ang landscape with mountains, water, trees, and buildings, all painted in a careful style with gold outlines and colorful use of blue and green. However, the hard, uninspired quality of the brush strokes would suggest again a Sung or even a Ming copy rather than an original by Li Chao-tao himself.

The landscape painter who by later critics, especially the followers of the so-called Southern School, was regarded as the greatest of all T'ang landscapists was Wang Wei, who was born in 699 and died in 759. Equally celebrated as a poet, whose lyrics are still widely read today, he has been throughout the ages one of the most famous of all Chinese artists. For a long time he was believed to be the author of an essay on landscape painting which bears his name, but modern scholars no longer think that he could have written it since it anticipates ideas which were not current until a later time.[27] He started his life as a court official but later retired to his country place, Wang Ch'uan in Shensi, where he lived alone, practicing Buddhist meditation and painting both Buddhist and landscape scrolls. According to the ninth-century critic Chu Ching-hsüan:

24

His paintings of landscapes, or of pines and rocks, were drawn like those of Master Wu (Tao-tzu) but were outstanding for their taste and nobility.... He did a picture of the Wang River, in which mountains and valleys, dense-crowded, twisted in and out, while clouds and water streamed by. His mind was beyond world-contamination, so that marvels grew from his brush-tip.... For his landscapes and his pines and rocks he too belongs in the wonderful class, top grade.[28]

Although no originals have been preserved, there is today a stone engraving of a copy of the Wang Ch'uan scroll mentioned above which may give some indication of his style *(Plate 8)*. Here again the quality of the copy is so poor that, in a literal sense, it is probably fairly close to the original. The rubbings extant today are made from a stone engraving by the Ming artist Kuo Shi-yüan, who in turn based his version upon a Sung copy which had been executed by Kuo Chung-shu.[29] Tradition has it that the original was also in monochrome, although other paintings by Wang Wei referred to in the art literature are described as being in color.[30] Thus, it seems likely that this scroll too had originally been painted in brilliant colors and that later critics, in order to have the master conform to their preconceived notions of what a work by the founder of the Southern School should have looked like, pretended that the Wang Ch'uan scroll had been painted in black and white. Certainly the difference between Wang Wei and his contemporaries was less great than the critics of the Ming period made it appear. In fact, a careful examination of these rubbings would suggest that the artist employed the same meticulous and detailed manner which was used by Li Chao-tao. The main difference, as far as one can see, is that Wang Wei emphasized the natural setting more and the buildings and figures less, suggesting that he was somewhat more advanced in the evolution of the pure landscape. The winding course of the river in the foreground, the towering mountain peaks with their many wrinkles, the variety of trees with their foliage making a pattern against the mountains, the tiny people, and in the center the equally tiny animals are all rendered with precise detail, and yet at the same time the artist achieves a far greater sense of unity in the design as a whole. Even more significant is the motif itself, that of the scholar's retreat amidst the beauty and solitude of nature, which is so close in spirit to the landscape painting of the Sung period. It may well be that Wang Wei's great influence on later artists can be explained by his new

25

conception of landscape painting, rather than by any technical innovation. Certainly there can be little doubt that the profound cleavage between the so-called Northern School, which followed the meticulous and colorful manner of Li Ssu-hsün, and the Southern School, with its freer style supposedly following the ink washes of Wang Wei, was very largely the creation of Ming scholars like Tung Ch'i-ch'ang, for neither in the painting nor the criticism of the T'ang period is there much sign of this difference.

Another famous Wang Wei composition was entitled "Clearing after Snowfall in the Hills by the River," of which two copies have come down to us. One is in the collection of Mr. Lo Chên-yü in Tientsin, and the other is owned by Professor Ogawa in Kyoto.[31] However, both of them are certainly no earlier than the Sung period, nor do they convey the spirit of the eighth century very convincingly. The subject is no doubt inspired by Wang Wei's celebrated painting and shows again what a great contribution the artist made towards the development of the landscape, for these are pure landscapes in which the figures no longer have an important place. At the same time, the execution cannot be faithful to the original, at least not if the scrolls were typical of Wang Wei, with the inspired brushwork traditionally associated with his name.

Many other works are either attributed to Wang Wei or are supposed to reflect his style, but most of them are not only poor in quality but have little similarity to anything which we associate with the period. Among these, the most convincing is a winter landscape, painted on silk with slight color, which is in the collection of the Freer Gallery (Plate 9). It is certainly a late copy, probably no earlier than the Ming period, but it seems to preserve the T'ang spirit pretty faithfully, especially in the lofty mountains, the gnarled trees, and the white snow. In fact, according to tradition, Wang Wei was particularly famous for his painting of snow-covered mountain tops, and many scrolls of this subject are still ascribed to him today.

A host of other works are either attributed to the masters of the T'ang period or said to be in the style of that age. Older publications were very apt to make such attributions upon the evidence of a signature or seal (which most of the time is obviously a later addition), without paying too much attention to the style of the actual painting. Many collectors of the earlier part of our century, such as the famous founder of the Freer Gallery, believed that they had dozens of original T'ang paintings, a number of them attributed to the most famous masters, but modern scholars have strongly disagreed. In fact, many of the more recent scholars have taken the opposite position, saying that no T'ang original could possibly have survived and that no positive attributions to individual artists can be made prior to the Yüan period. Both points of view seem rather extreme, for, although original T'ang works are few in number and the bulk of the rest are either provincial or more or less faithful copies, they do give some indication of what T'ang painting must have looked like.

One of these later copies, although certainly no earlier than Yüan or possibly Ming is nevertheless very interesting and may reflect a type common during the T'ang period. It belongs to the Metropolitan Museum in New York, to which it came from the former Bahr collection, and is entitled "Misty Landscape" and attributed to the T'ang painter Yang Shêng *(Plate 10)*.[32] The colors are bright and decorative, the mountains a brilliant bluish-green, the trees dark green and red, and the clouds white, with the brown of the silk creating a more subdued background. The style, with its emphasis upon areas of vivid color instead of individual brush strokes, is typical of a manner called "boneless painting," or *ku hua* in Chinese. In it, the linear accents and the calligraphic quality so important in most Chinese painting is subordinated to a colorful and decorative pattern. This kind of painting was far more common during the T'ang period than during the Sung, when the gentleman-painters of the Southern School neither admired it nor cared to imitate it. The emphasis in these works is less upon the mystery and majesty of nature or the expressiveness of the individual brush stroke than on the total pictorial effect. The rendering of atmosphere and space which in later works is so subtle and richly developed is, in the Metropolitan painting, still crude, with solid, clearly defined clouds and little or no suggestion of the haze so characteristic of later Chinese painting. Still, the design is pleasingly decorative, and although it is certainly a late and probably weak reflection of the original work by Yang Shêng, it helps us visualize a type of painting which must have been common during the eighth and the ninth centuries.

Another winter landscape which may well be a T'ang original is located in the Peking Palace Museum *(Plate 11)*. Some scholars have thought it to be by Wang Wei, but the very advanced style of the painting precludes such an attribution. However, its fine quality would suggest that this is an original by a hitherto unknown artist who probably was active during the last part of the T'ang period, presumably during the ninth century. If this is the case, the scroll would be of particular interest as a link between the eighth-century style of men such as Wang Wei and the style of the great landscapists of the early tenth century, the Five Dynasties period.[33] The simpler, looser style of painting in which bright colors and meticulous detail have given way to economy of means and the use of a few large forms suggests the later date. At the same time, the peculiar manner of painting, with its white highlights along the edges of the mountains and on the trunks and branches of the trees, the snowy roofs, and the tiny white figures, all contrasted with the dark surface of the silk, suggest a date prior to that of the mature monochrome landscapes of the tenth century. On the other hand, the mountains receding into the dark, mysterious sky create more feeling of space and atmosphere than had existed in earlier T'ang painting. The effect is certainly dramatic, and the complete subordination of the various little buildings and tiny figures to the soaring shapes of the mountains is a new development in the evolution of landscape painting.

Finally, at the periphery of the cultural world of the T'ang dynasty, there are two sites where genuine originals can be studied, one in the Buddhist caves at Tun Huang at the western fringes of the Chinese realm and the other in Japan at the Shōsō-in in Nara. Scholars differ over the question of the quality of the Tun Huang paintings, but there can be little doubt that they are provincial in character and do not represent the most advanced style of the capital. Still, they are originals of unquestioned authenticity, and they must reflect in some degree the painting of the period. Most interesting in connection with this study is the wall painting in cave Number 70, which shows a landscape dating from the seventh century.[34] In it the space is broken up into a series of small sections in which different episodes from Buddhist legends are represented. Figures and buildings dominate the scene, with the mountains and trees forming the same kind of incidental setting which was typical of the scroll paintings of the period. The drawing is precise, with a linear emphasis similar to that found in the work of Li Chao-tao, and while there is little space and atmosphere, there can be no doubt, if one compares this painting with the sixth-century landscape at the same site, that a marked advance in the rendering of the landscape had been made over the previous period.

Even more indicative of the prevailing artistic trends are the decorative objects which have been preserved since 756 in the Japanese Imperial Repository, the Shōsō-in, in Nara, and whose authenticity is beyond question. Although these are not major works, they are nevertheless of great interest for the light they shed upon the development of landscape painting.[35] The group in the Shōsō-in consists of screen panels, a wooden painted box, mirrors, and musical instruments called *biwa*'s, with landscapes painted on them. Of these, the most valuable for our purpose are the box and the *biwa*'s, for the screen panels are highly abstract and very archaic in character. The box cover, which is painted in gold and silver, has towering mountains, gnarled trees, and stylized clouds similar to those in the Li Chao-tao painting. The most striking of all, however, are the small landscapes on the plectrum guards, or *kambachi,* of the *biwa*'s, which show mountainous scenes with men and animals that are very close to the Peking Li Chao-tao and thus would appear to suggest that the scroll was done during this part of the T'ang period.

Limited as our knowledge of T'ang painting is, there nevertheless emerges, if we piece together the many fragments which have been considered here, the image of a definite T'ang style. The manner is one of precise and often beautifully rendered detail, and the brilliant colors, usually reds and greens and blues, create a rich and decorative pattern. The mountains have assumed a real importance, often towering to great heights against the sky, and other elements of landscape, such as clouds, rocks, trees, and rivers, appear in well-defined detail, but human figures as well as various types of buildings are still for the most part the chief center of interest. Towards the end of the period, nature begins to be dominant and there is a turning towards monochrome as a major medium, but more typical for the T'ang era are colorful paintings where man is the equal if not the measure of the mountains.

4

The Five Dynasties and
Early Sung Periods

THE age which has long been regarded, especially by the Yüan and the
Ch'ing critics, as the culmination of Chinese landscape painting was the
tenth century. Although it falls into two dynastic epochs, the Five Dynasties
period, extending from 907 to 960, and the early Sung period, which started
in 960, it forms, as far as the cultural development of China is concerned, a
unified whole. It was during this century that landscape painting made its
greatest strides and that the monochrome scroll of the type which had been
foreshadowed by the winter landscape in the Peking Palace Museum was
fully developed. Up to this time Buddhist and Taoist painting had been
equally important, but now landscape was supreme, and the emphasis upon
it led to one of the most glorious creative epochs in the history of Chinese
or, for that matter, any other art.

While the T'ang painters had always seen the landscape in relation to
human activity, the tenth-century artists created a pure landscape in which
the figures were subordinate to the natural setting. Their inspiration came
from nature, and many accounts tell how the painters of these magnificent
scrolls would wander for days in the wilderness, seeking inspiration among

the mountains and valleys, though their ambition was never to describe a particular scene but to interpret the spirit of nature itself, the mysterious essence which vitalizes the whole of creation. It would be wrong to call their landscapes realistic, yet at the same time, the term "ideal" would be just as inaccurate, for they are not classical in the sense that the term is applied to an artist like Poussin; they are, rather, based upon a particular experience of nature from which the artist has attempted to generalize, thus conveying the underlying spirit not of one landscape but of all.

Of the many magnificent scrolls which the artists of this period must have created, only a few have been preserved, and even among these the copies and later imitations no doubt far outnumber the originals. Since these painters enjoyed such a tremendous reputation during the Yüan period, it was only natural that their work should have been copied over and over again, sometimes, probably, with the intention of committing a fraud, but more frequently because the copyist wished to express his admiration for some painter of the glorious past.

The few surviving works which can be authenticated beyond any doubt, such as the wall paintings at Tun Huang and at Palin in eastern Mongolia, and the description of tenth-century paintings in the writings of the eleventh-century author Kuo Jo-hsü,[36] suggest that fundamental changes in landscape painting took place during this time. The contributions made by the celebrated artists of the period can hardly be exaggerated, being similar to those which the masters of the fifteenth century made in the development of Western art. Professor Bachhofer, in his valuable study of the rendering of space in Chinese painting of the first millenium, says that at this time, at the turn of the century, or the beginning of the Five Dynasties period, atmospheric effects such as clouds and fog are first used at Tun Huang in order to suggest depth, space, and atmosphere.[37] If one considers that these works are not only provincial but often of very poor quality, and if one allows for a certain cultural lag, there can be no doubt that these developments were already fully perfected in the capital. The eminent art critic Kuo Jo-hsü, who took up the story of Chinese painting where the T'ang critic Chang Yen-yüan left off in 841 and carried it through the year 1074, speaks of the same phenomenon when he praises the masters over and over again for their use of mist, clouds, space, and above all "atmospheric effect."

The first of the great painters of this age is Ching Hao, who was born during the last part of the T'ang dynasty and whose main artistic activity falls into the opening years of the tenth century. We are told that he was a great lover of nature and that he wandered about among the mountains to enjoy their solitude and grandeur. In the essay "Notes on Brushwork" attributed to him, he discusses the proper manner of painting landscapes:

As you like to paint clouds, forests, and landscapes, it is necessary for you to under-stand the origin of every phenomenon. Every tree grows according to its natural disposition. Pine trees may grow bent and crooked, but by nature they are never too crooked. They are sometimes densely and sometimes rather sparsely placed; they are neither green nor blue. They are upright from the beginning. Even as saplings their soul is not lowly, but their form is noble and solitary. Their branches may bend down and lie low, but they turn in an opposite direction and do not drop to the ground. Indeed, the pine trees in the forests are like the moral character of virtuous men, which is like the breeze. To paint them as soaring or coiling dragons with their branches and needles in confusion, therefore, is not at all in harmony with the spirit and rhythm of the pines.[38]

Unfortunately, little if any of Ching Hao's work survives today. Already in the eleventh century, the famous painter and collector Mi Fei, in his *Hua Shih,* was complaining that he had seen only two authentic works by Ching Hao, and the great Ming scholar and connoisseur Tung Ch'i-ch'ang also commented on the rarity of his work. Only two paintings are attributed to him today. One is the impressive scroll in the Peking Palace Museum entitled "View of the K'uan-lu Mountains" *(Plate 12),* and the other one is a landscape scroll in the collection of the Freer Gallery.[39] The latter, however, is very poorly preserved, and although traditionally associated with his name, it does not seem to have much connection with the style of the period. The Peking landscape, on the other hand, is of very fine quality and could well be either an original or a faithful copy of a Ching Hao painting. The somewhat hard and mechanical brushwork in the ridges of the mountain would make the latter the more likely alternative. On the whole, the style of the painting is in keeping with what we would expect to find during the period. The emphasis upon the height and massiveness of the towering mountains is characteristic of the age, yet the painting does

33

not show the feeling for depth and atmosphere which was considered the greatest achievement of the period. It is interesting to note that Kuo Jo-hsü lists Ching Hao with the T'ang painters[40] and that Mi Fei saw nothing very remarkable in his work and much preferred the painting of Fan K'uan, a master who lived later in the century.[41] There is a fine feeling in the scroll for the structure of the mountains and the growth of the trees, but the rendering of the space is still unconvincing. The forms are shown on several planes with a very definite foreground of trees at the right, a man and a boat in the center, and a body of water at the left. In the middle-ground there is another figure driving two donkeys down a road and, to his left, a house in front of steep cliffs and a waterfall; in the background immense mountains rear so high that they dominate the scroll. These various parts fail to form a unified whole, and the transitions from one plane to the next are not worked out with the skill which is found in later paintings. Nevertheless, the underlying conception which inspires the work, that of a natural world so overwhelming that it dwarfs man, is typical of the age and shows how, in spirit at least, Ching Hao marks the beginning of a new epoch in landscape painting.

A somewhat younger contemporary of Ching Hao's was Kuan T'ung, who was active during the first half of the tenth century. Although the catalogue of the imperial collection of Hui Tsung records no less than ninety-four of his landscapes, few of his works survive today. The most convincing of these is the large hanging scroll in the Peking Palace Museum entitled "The Ford of the Mountain Stream."[42] In contrast to the Ching Hao painting in the same collection, it would seem to be an original of the tenth century, for the brushwork is far more spontaneous and does not appear either dry or mechanical. The subject is again the familiar one of lofty mountains, trees, shrubs, houses, rocks, water, and tiny figures. However, the treatment of space and atmosphere shows a marked advance when compared to the Ching Hao scroll. The rocks and mountains give a far greater sense of both mass and depth, and by using mist and aerial perspective the artist has succeeded in conveying a true feeling of space. There can be no doubt that the art of landscape painting had evolved considerably during the few decades which separate these two painters.

34

The leading artist of the middle of the century, whose most important activity seems to have fallen into the opening years of the Sung dynasty, was Li Ch'êng, particularly famous for his winter landscapes and picturesque trees. According to Kuo Jo-hsü: "He was a most excellent painter of landscapes with wintry forests. His inspired versatility was the quintessence of the spiritual, very far beyond normal human [capacity]."[43] In an essay by the artist entitled "The Secrets of Landscape Painting," or *Shan Shui Chüeh,* he describes the proper methods of painting landscapes during different seasons:

The atmosphere of the mountain in spring is clear and charming; the trees in summer are thick and luxuriant; the autumnal forest is forlorn and solemn; and the winter trees are resigned and death-like. The roots of the trees should penetrate the soil like a dragon's claws gripping its prey. The stony ground is full of sharp edges, but its base is covered with soil.[44]

In another passage from this essay, Li Ch'êng discusses the importance of rendering depth and space properly:

In painting landscapes, one should decide first upon the positions of the host and guest mountains and then upon the relative distance of objects. After that he can mark out the scenery and the objects, and arrange the high and the low.[45]

Genuine works by Li Ch'êng were apparently already rare by the eleventh century, and Mi Fei laments the fact that he has only seen two authentic scrolls among more than three hundred imitations. Of those preserved today the most convincing is the hanging scroll in the Boston Museum of Fine Arts entitled "Travellers Among the Snowy Hills," which is already mentioned in Hui Hsung's *Catalogue of the Imperial Collection,* the *Hsüan Ho Hua P'u,* of 1120 *(Plates 13 and 14).* Painted on silk, it has suffered a good deal over the centuries, but it gives the impression of being an authentic work of the period. The subject, which is very similar to that painted by Ching Hao and Kuan T'ung, represents mountains, water, trees, buildings, and in the midst of the wild setting, a few miniature figures climbing up a mountain road. In contrast to the earlier paintings, this shows a somewhat different treatment of the background. Here the sky soars over the mountains, and to the right of the rocky mass there is a series of smaller ranges enveloped in haze which, as the quotation from the essay suggests, is used to indicate distance and space. The rendition of the trees, with their writhing branches, is typical of Li Ch'êng's manner of painting, as is the great economy of his brush stroke, which is brought out especially well in the detail of the travellers.

Another of Li Ch'êng's works, formerly in the Abe collection but now in the Osaka Museum, shows one of his most celebrated themes, that of a man on a mule in front of a memorial stele *(Plate 15)*. Although the figures are larger than they were in the winter landscape, the emphasis is less upon the man or the stele than upon the dragon-like forms of the gnarled trees. It must have been this kind of painting by Li Ch'êng which Mi Fei had in his collection and which he described in the following words:

The trunk thrusts upward in impressive display, the branches cast shadows by their exuberant growth. Where knot-holes are indicated, he has not [merely] used circles of ink, but instead has put one big blob at the bottom, and then has run across it lightly with a brush [holding] only pale ink. The result is a work of Heaven.[46]

It is this inspired quality of Li Ch'êng's brushwork which is praised again and again by later critics and which made him, especially in the eyes of the Yüan dynasty artists, one of the most renowned painters in the history of Chinese art.

Due to Li Ch'êng's great fame, there are many copies of his work, as well as paintings done in his manner, and there can be little doubt that the bulk of the scrolls which are today attributed to him fall into one or the other category. How faithfully they reflect his work is, of course, difficult to determine, since we have so little to go by, but there is a certain type of picturesque pine which from the Sung period on has been associated with him and is probably characteristic of his style. Among the many scrolls done in Li Ch'êng's manner, though probably not by the painter himself, one of the best is in the Nelson Gallery of Art in Kansas City *(Plate 16)*. Called "Buddhist Temple Amid Clearing Mountain Peaks," it has been traditionally ascribed to him, and although it does bear a good deal of resemblance to the kind of subject he painted as well as to his style, the hard quality of the brush strokes, especially in the buildings and the waterfall, would suggest that it is a Yüan copy rather than a Sung original.

The culminating artistic figure of this age was Tung Yüan, who worked during the last decades of the tenth century. According to the commentators of the eleventh century, who must have had the opportunity to see many of his works since the Imperial Catalogue of Hui Tsung lists no less than seventy-eight paintings by him, he was noted for his treatment of atmosphere and space. Mi Fei said of him:

Tung Yüan's level, pale [passages] are full of Heaven's truth; no T'ang [master] has such quality.... His peaks and ranges emerge and disappear; clouds and mist now reveal, now obscure. Here are no tricked-out ingenuities; in everything he has caught the very truths of Heaven. In the line of his vapors with their streaming azure, in strong out-thrusting of his branches and trunks, one feels everywhere a sense of life itself. His mountain streams with their bridges and fishing reaches, his shadowed islets, are a very slice of Kiangnan.[47]

Another eleventh-century critic, Shên Kua, describes his style in these words:

Tung Yüan was a skillful painter of autumn mists and distant scenery. He mostly painted the actual hills of Kiangnan and did not draw upon his imagination for marvellous cliffs. Later on came the Buddhist priest Chü-jan, who took Tung Yüan as his model, and succeeded in mastering the same principles of beauty. The work of these two painters must be seen from a distance, on account of the roughness of their brushwork. Seen close, the objects in their pictures seem almost shapeless masses, but when held at a distance, the scenery and general details stand brilliantly out, stirring profound emotions and suggesting far-away thoughts, as though one were gazing upon some strange land.[48]

It would appear that Tung Yüan, coming about a century after Ching Hao, had completely mastered the effects of cloudy space, and thus was able to evoke distance and far-off views convincingly. Although his work undoubtedly comes as the culmination of a long development which can ultimately be traced back to T'ang times, the critics seem to have felt that he was a great innovator who, around the year 1000, perfected the Sung landscape style. According to Kuo Jo-hsü, the artist worked both in the monochrome manner first used by Wang Wei and in the colored style of Li Ssu-hsün, but it was upon the so-called wet-ink monochromes that his fame primarily rested.[49]

Among the works attributed to him, by far the best, and indeed, one of the greatest Chinese scrolls which has survived, is a painting in the Boston

Museum of Fine Arts *(Plates 17, 18, and 19)*. Called "A Clear Day in the Valley," it is the section of a larger scroll originally entitled "Rivers and Hills in Wind and Rain," but unfortunately the other parts have disappeared. Painted in ink on paper with only slight coloring, it is very simple, and though small, it is one of the most impressive landscape paintings of all times. It carries the signature of the artist as well as an encomium by the well-known Ming critic Tung Ch'i-ch'ang dated 1633 and stating that this is a genuine work by Tung Yüan. This opinion is of particular value, not only because Tung Ch'i-ch'ang was such a distinguished connoisseur but also because he had presumably seen many originals by tenth-century painters and so was in a far better position to judge their authenticity than we are today. There are some modern critics, both Chinese and Western, who tend to doubt this attribution and believe that on stylistic grounds the scroll should be ascribed to the twelfth or even the fourteenth century. The main reason they advance is that the atmospheric quality of the vaporous distance would not be found in a tenth-century work. However, since it is this very quality which critics living only a century later praised in his work, and since he was felt to have been a great innovator, there seems to be no valid reason for rejecting the attribution based upon the judgment of such an eminent critic as Tung Ch'i-ch'ang.

Everything that the earlier tenth-century artists had been striving for is here perfectly expressed, and the result is a painting of almost magic power. The scroll opens with wonderful mountain scenery rendered with many subtle brush strokes and delicate tonal effects *(Plate 17)*. The repeated wrinkles, or *ts'un,* of the mountain folds suggest shading and modelling and thus achieve a strong feeling of solidity. On the crests there are small pines, and scattered around the trunks, dots, or *tien,* which represent moss and grass. In the foreground are trees, beautifully painted, and water, and a little retreat which a man and his servant are about to enter. Directly behind are the mountains looming grandly above the house and in the background, some distant peaks are seen dimly through the haze. Every brush stroke is meaningful and expressive, subtle and yet firm. The ink wash itself is employed in many gradations, giving a beautiful variety of tones.

The second section shows a view of a lake with hills extending into

38

the water *(Plate 18)*. There are also trees, a boat, some figures, and rising above the fog, a range of distant mountains. Here, in the soft and subtle tone of the ink wash in the background, one sees the inspired skill of the artist in rendering atmosphere, a skill which heightens the theme of man lost in the immensity of nature. This feeling finds perfect expression in the last part of the scroll, where the foreground is nearly filled by the lake, delicately suggested by the paper itself *(Plate 19)*. Only a narrow finger of land extends into the water, and in the distance a line of hills emerges from the enveloping fog. Almost lost in the boundless space, there are three men who stand at the edge of the water and wait for the ferry, which works its way slowly towards the travellers. These figures are so tiny in relation to the setting that at first glance they might be taken for something else, and their very smallness suggests, by contrast, the infinite wonder of the Tao. Certainly in a painting like this, the whole spirit underlying Chinese landscape painting finds its supreme expression.

Of the other works attributed to Tung Yüan the most convincing, although perhaps only a close copy done at a somewhat later time, is the one in the Peking Palace Museum entitled "Cave of the Immortals" *(Plate 20)*. In contrast to the Boston scroll, this is painted in color and lacks the inspired subtlety of the former. However, since we are specifically told that Tung Yüan worked in both manners, it is quite possible that these works are by the same artist. If this be the case, it would then seem that the Peking landscape was an earlier work closer in style to the T'ang age, while the Boston scroll may be from the period of his artistic maturity, when the Sung manner had been fully developed. The somewhat dry, uninspired quality of the Peking painting may well be due to the fact that this is a close copy rather than an original.

The theme is again the familiar one of the mountain landscape with a body of water, trees, buildings, and tiny figures. The view is somewhat different insofar as the landscape is seen from a high point in the foreground rather than from a level position or looking up from below. This is done so that the artist may show receding groups of mountains and thus increase the illusion of space and distance. However, when compared with the Boston scroll, it is far less subtle, with the contours seeming too sharp and with none of the atmospheric quality in which, according to Chinese critics, Tung Yüan excelled. At the same time, the general scheme is similar, with trees in the foreground and a large mountain with smaller ones dominating the right half of the picture, while the left is filled with water and distant mountains. It would thus seem quite possible that we have here an early and a late work by the same artist.

A painter who, in all accounts, is closely linked with Tung Yüan and was apparently a follower of his is the monk Chü-jan. The exact dates of his life are not known, but it is believed that he was slightly younger than his teacher and was active during the last years of the tenth century. He too was much admired by later painters and critics, especially those of the Yüan period. Kuo Jo-hsü in describing his work calls him "a skillful landscape painter, whose brush and ink were fair and moistly-rich. He was good at doing misty atmospheric effects, and high spacious views of mountains and rivers; forest trees, however, were not his strong point."[50] The Imperial Catalogue of Hui Tsung lists no less than one hundred and thirty-six of his landscapes and says:

He had a profound [sense of what was] of exceptional interest.... Whenever he set down his brush, it was like some author or man of parts at the moment of composing in poetical form; a veritable spring would gush forth in abundance from the tip of his brush...the great riches within his breast gave an inexhaustible fertility to his brush. Chü-jan's landscapes beyond their peaks and ranges and gorges, will descend by way of wooded foothills; there he will set such things as big boulders, pine and cypress, scattered bamboo, vines and grasses, all helping to bring each other out. His somber ravines with their tiny trails dipping and turning, winding and enclosing; his bamboo fences and thatched huts, his high-hung bridges and perilous cause-ways, are as real as actual mountain scenery.[51]

There are many paintings to which his name is attached, but it seems doubtful that any are by the artist himself. Most of them look as if they are at best Yüan paintings in the style of Chü-jan. Of all the works attributed to him, the most convincing is a mountain landscape in the Peking Palace Museum,[52] but even this seems closer in spirit to Yüan painting than what we know of the work of the late tenth century. The general impression which the picture creates is that Chü-jan was similar to Tung Yüan but softer and weaker, with little of the expressive strength of the older master.

40

However, this scroll may not give an adequate idea of what the style of Chü-jan was really like. Another painting which in some of the older books has been linked with his name is the beautiful Yangtze River landscape in the Freer Gallery, but most critics today agree that it could not possibly be of such an early date.

The last and one of the greatest in this group of early Sung painters was Fan K'uan, who was probably born during the second half of the tenth century but lived into the eleventh, for we are told that he was still alive during the T'ien Shêng era (1023—1032). Mi Fei, in describing his work, says:

In his usual style he loved to do dense forests on the crests of his mountains; [in these] there is an advance beyond [his early] stage in respect to [signs of] decay and age. At the water's edge, [again] he would do big rocks jutting straight up; [here] there is an advance in strength and hardness. I am confident that he was a pupil of Ching Hao.[53]

His fame was so great that he was considered the equal of Li Ch'êng and Kuan T'ung, and he was thought to surpass all of his contemporaries.

Of the works ascribed to him, by far the most impressive is a mountain landscape in the Peking Palace Museum *(Plate 21)*. Here one sees the full mastery of the mature early-Sung style, and there can be little doubt that this is an original by one of the great artists of Chinese painting. The dominant motif is once again the mountains, immense, majestic, dwarfing everything else in the painting. But what makes the work so beautiful is the way in which the artist suggests the mist that partially surrounds the mountains, without sacrificing any of their solidity. In the foreground, in front of the building, the tiny figure sitting beneath the tree is almost invisible, a mere speck in the midst of overwhelming grandeur. As his critics maintained, Fan K'uan was indeed able to express the very spirit of the mountains.

Another work attributed to Fan K'uan but inferior in quality is the hanging scroll "Mountains with Palaces in Snow," in the Boston Museum of Fine Arts *(Plate 22)*. The style of this painting as well as the composition is quite similar to the scroll in Peking, but the execution is uninspired, with over-elaborate, mechanical brush strokes, suggesting that we have a later

41

copy after a work by Fan K'uan, if indeed this painting can be connected with the artist at all. The treatment of the trees and the lesser emphasis upon the mist and atmosphere is closer to Li Ch'êng, and it is possible that this scroll was an early work or a copy of one, for we are told that he was a close follower of the older master.

There are numerous other hanging scrolls with mountain landscapes painted in this manner and using a similar composition, some of them with famous names attached and others by anonymous artists. Most of them are undoubtedly Yüan and Ming paintings in the style of the early-Sung masters since these later artists greatly admired their predecessors and often worked in their manner. Among these, one of the most interesting, although poorly preserved, is a mountain landscape in ink with white pigment and faint color in the Nelson Gallery in Kansas City (Plate 23). It is impossible to identify the painting as the work of one particular artist, but its style certainly fits into the late tenth century, and it is in all likelihood an original or a very close copy of one.

An interesting painting from the same period, the authenticity of which cannot be doubted, is the "Autumn Scene" painted on the wall of a Liao tomb at Palin in eastern Mongolia (Plate 24).[54] This is one of four such scenes representing the seasons and executed around 1033, and no doubt a provincial reflection of a somewhat earlier style. The brightly-colored trees and the deer, as well as the linear accents and rather shallow space, are similar, although much inferior in quality, to the famous deer-park scrolls in the Peking Palace Museum, which are traditionally ascribed to the Five Dynasties.[55] Certainly these wall paintings are a proof that, even in the far-flung outposts of the Chinese cultural world, landscape painting had already reached maturity by this time.

5

The Northern Sung Period

THE eleventh century built upon the foundations provided by the artistic developments of the tenth, and the result was a flowering of Chinese painting in general, and the landscape in particular, which has seldom been equalled and certainly never surpassed in the history of art. Kuo Hsi was the outstanding painter of this period: such was the opinion of Kuo Jo-hsü in 1074,[56] a verdict with which later critics would readily agree. As he was born in 1020 and died in 1090, the main part of his artistic career falls into the second half of the eleventh century, during which time he was the leading painter-scholar at the Imperial Academy of Painting. His extraordinary fame rests as much upon his literary activities as on his painting for, as we had seen above, his essay on landscape painting entitled *Lin Ch'üan Kao Chih,* or "The Lofty Message of Forests and Streams," is probably the most famous of all Chinese writings on the art of landscape painting. In it his own thoughts on the subject as well as the more general philosophy of landscape painting are discussed. In writing about the different seasons and how they are reflected in nature, he says:

Spring and summer views of the mountains have certain aspects; autumn and winter views have others. That is to say, the scenery of the four seasons is not the same. The morning view of the mountain has its own appearance, the evening its own; views on a clear day or cloudy day still their own. That is to say, the morning and evening views of the mountains are not the same. Thus, views of a single mountain combine in themselves the changes and significances of several thousand mountains.[57]

A perfect expression of this, and one of the finest Chinese paintings in America, is the hand scroll in the Freer Gallery of Art entitled "An Autumn Day in the Valley of the Yellow River" *(Plates 25 and 26)*. Here, developed to their utmost, are all the elements which make these landscapes so beautiful —the mountains, the pines, the river, the waterfall, the houses hidden beneath the trees, the solitary hermit, and above all, the wonderful feeling for mist obscuring the forms and creating an illusion both of aerial perspective and space. As Kuo Hsi says:

A mountain viewed at close range has one appearance, a mountain viewed at a distance of several miles has another. When viewed from a distance of scores of miles it has still another. The change of appearance caused by the varying degree of distance from the object is figuratively known as "the change of shape with every step one takes."[58]

The eye of the onlooker is, in these scrolls, drawn into space so that the lover of landscape may imagine himself wandering through the scenery as it unrolls before him. The picture is painted in subtle ink tones which create a beautiful feeling of mysteriousness and, at the same time, peace. It is an art based upon the natural scene, yet it is not naturalistic in the nineteenth-century sense, for the artist has expressed through one valley of one river the spirit of all such valleys, and it is because of this that these paintings have their lasting appeal.

Other outstanding works by Kuo Hsi are the two hanging landscape scrolls in the Palace Museum in Peking, which continue the tradition of men such as Fan K'uan but have a fantastic quality which give them a character of their own. They are also freer and more dynamic than the relatively massive and static landscapes of the earlier painters, thus indicating a development towards greater boldness, as the art of landscape painting reached its full development. Many other works have at one time or another been associated with this illustrious name, but there seems little reason for considering that any of them are originals.

The other outstanding artist of the second half of the eleventh century is Mi Fei, who was born in 1051 and died in 1107. He too held various

44

official positions and was famous not only as a painter but as a critic, writer, and calligrapher. His well-known *Hua Shih,* or *History of Painting,* reveals him to be a distinguished connoisseur who himself owned a celebrated collection of Chinese paintings. His great prestige was partially due to his being considered an outstanding exponent of the Southern School, which later critics regarded so highly, and his influence was considerable, with many later artists working in the style which he first employed.

As he himself said, Mi Fei particularly loved landscapes which have haze, clouds, and mist. Among those still attributed to him, the finest are the ones in the Freer Gallery and the Peking Palace Museum. The first, called "Misty Landscape," bears Mi Fei's seal and signature *(Plate 27)*. Although it is in poor condition and has obviously been repaired and repainted, it is, even today, one of the really great Chinese paintings. The emphasis is no longer upon lines or individual brush strokes; instead, the artist employs loosely-applied ink washes, and yet the painting loses nothing of its structure. The rounded mountain tops emerging from a sea of haze have none of the detail so characteristic of earlier painting. Wrinkles, trees, moss are all indicated in the simplest way, and in the foreground the groups of trees dark against the mist are so generalized that the leaves and branches and trunks are merged together.

The Peking painting is equally outstanding and also bears the seal and signature of the artist *(Plate 28)*. This time there is a more linear emphasis in the pines in the foreground and in the very abstractly rendered pavilion, but the dominant theme is still the mountain peaks, which rise from a haze that completely obscures the middle-ground of the painting. The composition in both works is extremely simple. Everything is rendered economically, with the various forms reduced to their essentials and man represented by tiny, isolated buildings, which, by their loneliness, increase the poetic mood of the paintings. Another work attributed to Mi Fei is the landscape with fog in the Nakamura collection in Tokyo, which is similar in style to the other two and also carries his signature and the date 1102.[60]

Among the many artists who continued Mi Fei's style, the most important one during the Northern Sung period was undoubtedly his son, Mi Yu-jên, who lived from 1086 to 1165. A good example of his work may be seen in the Freer Gallery, a hand scroll of a misty mountain and river scene *(Plates 29 and 30)*. The emphasis on the haze is like that in the work of the elder Mi and so is the extreme simplicity of the composition, but the son's painting lacks the strength and solidity which characterized the work of his father. The forms seem to dissolve into the haze, and the artist does not create much illusion of the massiveness and structure of the mountains. Another example by Mi Yu-jên, dated 1130 and located in the Cleveland Museum of Art, has similar stylistic traits but is less well preserved.[61]

An excellent original from the eleventh century which so far cannot be connected with the work of any one particular artist is a painting in the collection of the Metropolitan Museum in New York called "Tribute Horse" *(Plate 31)*. In contrast with the other paintings considered from this period, there is color in the scroll and a greater emphasis on the figures and horses, both of which are traits closer to the T'ang style. Nevertheless, the perfect control of the spatial treatment and the soft rendition of the beautiful pine in the foreground would suggest a date no earlier than the beginning of the eleventh century. Certainly the author of this splendid work was no ordinary painter, for the quality of the brush strokes, the harmoniously balanced composition, and the subtle use of color are worthy of one of the ranking artists of the period. Since the horsemen move from right to left and there is at both ends a suggestion of a continuation of the composition, it seems likely that this is merely a part of a larger scroll, the rest of which has vanished. Perhaps some day it will be possible to link this scroll with one of the many artists whose names are recorded but of whom no known works have been preserved.

The two most famous artists of the first half of the twelfth century, the end of the Northern Sung period and the beginning of the Southern Sung, were Li T'ang and Chao Po-chü. Although both were already prominent during the rule of the Emperor Hui Tsung, they moved to Hang-chou, where the Sung rulers sought refuge when the Northern capital was conquered in 1126 by the Jurchen Tungus tribes which established the Chin dynasty. However, since both had matured during the Northern Sung period, they are here considered as part of the earlier tradition, which, in fact, was carried on during the early part of the Southern Sung reign. Actually, the political

46

and military defeats of the Chinese empire had surprisingly little effect upon the culture of the time, which, in spite of these disasters, continued to be one of brilliant creativity.

Li T'ang, the earlier of the two, who was probably born around the middle of the eleventh century, has been known traditionally for his paintings of water buffaloes and for genre scenes from village life.[62] However, in recent times a new aspect of his work was revealed by the discovery of his signature upon a picture formerly ascribed to Wu Tao-tzu.[63] The painting is one of a pair of hanging scrolls of summer and winter in the collection of the Kōtō-in in Kyoto *(Plate 32)*.[64] It is believed by some scholars that there were originally four pictures representing the seasons, a subject common to Chinese painting. The summer scene is the one which bears the signature, although there can be no doubt that both are by the same artist. Their style is certainly similar to that of the twelfth century, and the attribution to Li T'ang seems convincing. Since he was the most famous of the artists who served at the imperial court, it is of great interest for us to have, at last, a landscape with his signature. The economy and freedom of the brush stroke and the expressive power of the paintings are certainly worthy of one of the leading figures of the Sung period, and stylistically, too, it is most convincing to place these scrolls between the more meticulous manner of a eleventh-century painter such as Kuo Hsi and the great thirteenth-century masters of the Southern Sung period such as Hsia Kuei and Ma Yüan, who use an even freer and more suggestive style.

The summer scene represents a beautiful mountain landscape with a tiny figure carrying a heavy bundle in the background. Between precipitous mountains, a stream curves into the foreground and, balancing the tall, narrow peaks which rise beyond the pass, a group of trees stands on a rocky bank *(Plate 33)*. The detail of the trees brings out the quality of the brush strokes, vigorous and slashing in the claw-like roots, the snaky branches, the fantastic trunks, less linear in the leaves, and skillfully controlled in the pine needles and the grass. The theme itself is typical of the ideals of the landscape as set forth by Kuo Hsi, for it represents a particular time of year and reveals a mood associated with the season. The winter scroll is similar in spirit, conjuring up a feeling of desolation and barrenness, and in both the paintings

47

the treatment of the rocks in the foreground and the twisting branches and trunks foreshadow in their boldness and power the style which was to become dominant in the thirteenth century.

Another group of landscape paintings traditionally ascribed to this period is the set of hanging scrolls which since the Ashikaga period have been attributed to the Emperor Hui Tsung. One of the four works, that depicting spring, is lost, while the autumn *(Frontispiece)* and winter landscapes are now in the collection of the Konchi-in in Kyoto and the summer landscape is owned by the Kuon-ji near Mt. Minobu. Judging from the style of the paintings, which is quite advanced and bears striking resemblance to the works of some of the Southern Sung artists such as Ma Yüan, it seems most unlikely that these paintings are quite as early as this. It appears more probable that they were painted during the middle of the twelfth century by an unknown artist, for they form a transition from the work of masters such as Li T'ang to that of the great Southern Sung painters and combine features of both styles.

A very different kind of artist is the slightly younger Chao Po-chü, who was the favorite painter of the first ruler of the Southern Sung realm, Kao Tsung. Unlike the other Northern Sung painters we have considered (with the exception of the anonymous artist of the "Tribute Horse"), he worked mainly in the *ch'ing lü pai* manner, in which brilliant blues and greens and golden outlines are used. This type of painting goes back to the T'ang painter Li Ssu-hsün, who, with his followers, had employed meticulous brush strokes and bright colors, achieving a gay and decorative effect. It was a style considered typical of the Northern School and thus was scorned by the scholars of the Yüan and Ming periods, but it still persisted over the centuries, and during the Ming age it had such an outstanding exponent as Ch'iu Ying.

Among the many works attributed to Chao Po-chü, most of which are of elaborate palaces in mountain landscapes, the most impressive is a long scroll in the Boston Museum of Fine Arts entitled "Entry of the First Emperor of the Han Dynasty into Kuan Chung" *(Plate 34)*. It has the artist's signature and a dedication which suggests that it was presented to the Emperor Kao Tsung. The detail reproduced shows the armies of the Han emperor travelling through the mountains, but instead of painting individual soldiers, the artist concentrates upon the banners fluttering in the wind and suggests the presence of an army by the large tent in the upper left and a smaller one in the middle, where a soldier is sitting on the ground beside his flag. There is another figure in the left foreground, and in the center some unsaddled horses, making a decorative group with their curved necks and different colors. The main emphasis, however, is upon the scenery, with willows arched gracefully over a waterfall and a beautiful pine surrounded by tall and narrow poplars. The mountains are a blue-green with delicate gold lines, and behind the dark green trees there is a cloud, large and flat with little scalloped edges. It is used as one of the elements of the design and, together with the flags and trees and mountains, makes a pattern beautiful as decoration, though it lacks the mysterious quality which marked the work of Mi Fei.

Another scroll attributed to Chao Po-chü, one in the Metropolitan Museum entitled "Spring Morning at the Palace of the Han Emperors," is certainly in his style, although possibly it is a later copy instead of an original *(Plate 35).*[66] The subject is from ancient history, and the emphasis is more upon the splendid palace architecture than upon the grandeur of nature. The colors, like those in the Boston painting, are bright and decorative, with blue-green in the rocks and mountains, red in the palace, dark green and pink in the trees, white in the clouds, and gold for the outlines, all seen against a yellow-brown which adds to the warmth and beauty of the whole. It is painted in a very precise style, one which the Chinese refer to as *kung pi,* and here again there are beautifully rendered trees, overhanging pines and graceful willows, flowering fruit trees and elegant palms. In the splendid setting there are some figures standing on the terrace, but they are not emphasized, appearing merely as tiny parts subordinate to the whole.

The Northern Sung period in spite of its disastrous record in the political and military administration of the country, was a time of tremendous cultural activity, in which the art of the landscape reached new and splendid heights. Although there was an underlying unity both of style and outlook, there was at the same time a great diversity which is best seen in the work of such different artists as Kuo Hsi, Mi Fei, Li T'ang, and Chao Po-chü. This creativity, far from subsiding after the loss of northern China by the Sung rulers, continued and even increased, suggesting that perhaps because of the political decline the creative energies of the nation were channeled into the production of great art.

6

The Southern Sung Period

THE upsets accompanying the defeat of Hui Tsung and the loss of northern China to the foreign invaders only disrupted the artistic activities for a short time. The new capital at Hang-chou became almost at once the center of culture, the Imperial Academy was re-established, and leading Northern Sung painters such as Li T'ang and Chao Po-chü transferred their activities to the Southern Sung court and became great favorites. However, the artistic developments which were to prove the glory of this period did not take place until the last part of the century, when a school of monochrome landscape painting emerged which has been considered, particularly in Japan and in the West, as the climax of Chinese painting. The tendencies which had appeared in such scrolls as the winter landscape now attributed to Li T'ang came to their fullest development around the year 1200, and the result was a school of painting which produced some of the greatest artists the world has ever known.

Strangely enough, the Chinese themselves never regarded the work of this school with the admiration it so richly deserves, although during the Sung period itself and also during the Ming period, it had a considerable reputation and exerted a great influence upon the artists of the day. The reason for this neglect on the part of Chinese scholars and critics was due to the fact that the leading painters, Ma Yüan and Hsia Kuei, were considered members of the Northern in contrast to the Southern School, which enjoyed the greater prestige among Chinese scholars. This was because the Southern School alone was thought to be the proper precursor of the "literary men's painting," or the *wên jên hua,* of the scholar-artist of later times, which was the ideal of the writers and artists of the Ming and Ch'ing periods. Actually the motivation for classing some painters in the one school and some in the other is not based so much upon stylistic criteria as on the question of whether the artists were professionals or gentlemen-painters, the latter being the ones who were most admired.

The result of this was that the works of these artists were not as ardently sought after as those of the Southern School, and therefore the Japanese scholars and collectors who, especially during the Ashikaga period, vastly admired these painters were able to acquire some of their finest scrolls. The most famous of the collections assembled during this period were those of the Shoguns Yoshimitsu and Yoshimasa, which today are unfortunately dispersed.[67] The Japanese have always shown much more care in preserving their artistic treasures than the Chinese, and the result has been that some of the masterpieces of Chinese painting are found in Japan. In more recent years American collections have also acquired some outstanding works, so that the knowledge and appreciation of Southern Sung painting has been further enhanced. It must be added that the West was first introduced to Chinese painting through the magnificent Japanese publications which were put out in the early years of our century and that, because of this, a wave of enthusiasm for Southern Sung landscape painting swept Europe and America.

The two greatest members of the school were Ma Yüan and Hsia Kuei, both of whom were active during the last decades of the twelfth and the first decades of the thirteenth century. The exact dates of their lives are not known, an indication of the neglect which they suffered from Chinese writers and critics, but modern scholars believe they were born around the middle of the twelfth century. We are told that Ma Yüan became a member of the Academy during the reign of the Emperor Kuan Tsung (1190—1194). He also received the Golden Girdle, and it is recorded that he was still active during the reign of Li Tsung (1225—1264) but that he died before the middle of the century. Hsia Kuei is supposed to have worked during the reign of the Emperor Ning Tsung (1195—1224) and, according to reports, he also held the Golden Girdle and was a member of the Academy. Little else seems to be known about the lives of these painters except that Ma Yüan was the descendant of a long line of artists in the Ma family; his father, grandfather, and great-grandfather, as well as his brother and his son were likewise painters. It is also reported that Hsia Kuei had studied the works of Fan K'uan, Tung Yüan, and Mi Fei and that he was a follower of Li T'ang, whose landscapes indeed resemble his own.[68]

Most characteristic of the work of Ma Yüan, both in style and composition as well as mood and subject matter, is a hanging scroll entitled "Moonlit Night" in the Kuroda collection in Tokyo (Plate 36). The motif is the typical one of the sage seated beneath an overhanging pine as he contemplates the moon. It has often been suggested by Western critics that the spirit of these works is a romantic one like that of the painters and poets of the nineteenth century. This, however, is false, for the feeling expressed here is not the individualistic and deeply emotional one of the Romantics but rather a Taoist pantheism where the sage, far from emphasizing his individuality, seeks to negate it by merging himself with the serenity of nature. Thus, in the Ma Yüan scroll, the figures, instead of creating a mood through their own personalities, help to sustain the mood set by the landscape.

The style of the painting is beautifully adapted to the depth of the underlying thought, for the artist has employed the simplest means, using just the yellow silk and the monochrome ink washes with no color, no dynamic rhythm or violent contrast. The subtle and expertly handled brush alone contains the secret of his mastery. In the detail of the middle part of the painting, every stroke is applied with such strength and expressiveness that none could be added and none could be taken away (Plate 37). This economy is typical of the artist's style, and the composition is also very characteristic, showing the unilateral or, as the Chinese call it, "side-horned" design, in which the main weight of the forms is at one side. Yet by subtle compositional devices such as the introduction of the branch with the moon above it and in the foreground the heavy rock, the little boy, and the fence, a delicate balance is achieved, despite the apparent emphasis on the left side of the painting. This same composition is often used by the Japanese print-makers, and at the end of the nineteenth century it was introduced into the West, where it is found in the work of artists like Whistler.

Of the paintings by Ma Yüan in American collections, the finest is probably the album leaf called "Bare Willows and Distant Mountains" in the Boston Museum of Fine Arts *(Plate 38)*, which also owns several other paintings attributed to Ma Yüan. In this work, as in the "Moonlit Night," one sees the same extraordinary control, at once so simple and expressive. The two willows in the foreground are particularly fine, with single strokes, sometimes continuous and sometimes disconnected, used to draw the branches, from which hang delicately drooping twigs. The willows are too generalized to be realistic, yet with a few simple strokes, Ma Yüan has distilled their essence. They dominate the foreground and at the same time lead into the picture, the diagonal of the lower starting towards the bridge and then, as the branch rises, hanging over the buildings on the other side of the river. In the background a few simply rendered mountains stand against the sky which, like other areas of the painting, is done by leaving much of the silk empty, a device which suggests a mysterious and endless space. In the lower right there is the tiny figure of a traveller, minute in scale and yet painted with the same wonderful economy in which, with several strokes, a complete figure is created.

Another Ma Yüan painting which has recently entered an American collection is the long hand scroll entitled "The Four Sages of Shang Shan" in the Cincinnati Art Museum. The subject itself is already characteristic of the ideals of the period, for the painting represents the four sages of ancient times who, during the turmoils and barbarism of the Chin rule, retreated into the mountain wilderness and there led a life worthy of the true sage. The section reproduced shows two of them playing chess, while a third watches as he leans on the trunk of a slanted tree *(Plate 39)*. Rocks and twisted branches fill the rest of the painting, and here again Ma Yüan succeeds in rendering them without losing himself in a wealth of naturalistic detail.

There is at least one other work which should be mentioned in any discussion of the artist, and that is the famous scroll of the fisherman on the winter lake, formerly in the collection of Baron Mitsui and now in the Tokyo National Museum.[69] All the picture shows is the lonely figure of an angler seated at the edge of a boat, a few lines representing waves, and the vast expanse of the water indicated by the yellow silk. Rarely has such economy of means created such a moving effect, and it is in a work like this that the true greatness of Ma Yüan and the depth of his insight into the nature of reality are revealed in their most perfect form.

Ma Yüan's contemporary and rival, Hsia Kuei, is equal to him in genius, and some critics believe that he even surpasses Ma Yüan. Magnificent examples of his work have been preserved in China itself as well as in Japan and America. Perhaps the most beautiful of all his paintings is the summer scene in the collection of Baron Iwasaki in Tokyo, which was probably once the segment of a larger scroll *(Plate 40)*. The soft beauty of the ink wash against the silk, the subtle rendering of the mountains emerging from the mist, the single boat silhouetted against the fog-obscured lake, the fisherman's hut, the trees, the rocks, the tiny figure crossing the bridge all show a mastery seldom equalled. Certainly the great tradition of Chinese landscape painting which had found such an eloquent spokesman in Kuo Hsi centuries before has here come to a climax which later artists could not sustain. Western critics have compared these works of Hsia Kuei to the wash drawings of Rembrandt and there is certainly a similarity between the technique and the artistic control of the two, but the Chinese artist had a profound insight into nature and a personal relationship to it which the Dutch painter lacked.

Of the Hsia Kuei paintings in America, by far the most outstanding, in fact, in this author's opinion, one of the three most beautiful scrolls in the United States (the others being the Kuo Hsi in the Freer and the Tung Yüan in Boston) is the "Mountain and Lake Landscape" in the Nelson Gallery in Kansas City *(Plates 41, 42, and 43)*. Several versions of this painting are in existence, but there can be little doubt that the Kansas City one alone is by the master himself. The subtlety of the tonal effects, the firmness and inspired quality of the brush strokes, the economy as well as the beauty of the whole could only have been created by Hsia Kuei. Various scenes are shown, but all of them express the same mood, that of a peace so profound that it has something of a religious quality. Most moving of all, perhaps, is the part which shows the lake with the line of the shore barely visible in

55

the mist. There are three tiny, faceless figures in a long narrow boat and at the right some rushes extending into the water. Most of the surface of the silk is empty, suggesting the loneliness and mystery of the ultimate Tao better than any details or color could ever do.

Of the album leaves by Hsia Kuei in America, the finest is the one in the Boston Museum called "Sailboat in the Rain" *(Plate 44)*. Although it is badly damaged, it still has all the indications of an original by Hsia Kuei, for it shows the same subtle beauty of tone and brush so characteristic of the painter. Instead of a calm, peaceful landscape, we have here a more dramatic scene of trees in a rainstorm, with branches and leaves blowing in the wind. On the water is a boat with full sails, and in the distance the edge of the mountain peaks are just discernible in the rainy air. Hsia Kuei has compressed into a small format the feeling of the majesty of nature, and the little boat, driven before the wind, symbolizes man's place in the universe.

Of the paintings in China, certainly the best is one called "River, Mountains and Trees" in the National Museum in Peking.[70] In this long scroll, the artist represents a river landscape in his characteristic style, and the superb quality of the work leaves little doubt that it is an original. The same probably cannot be said for the other famous Peking Hsia Kuei scroll, one in the Palace Museum which is called "A Myriad Miles of the Yangtze";[71] its uninspired and often weak brushwork would suggest a later copy rather than an original. Numerous other scrolls and album leaves, both in American and Japanese collections, are attributed, with more or less justice, to the artist, and many of them are of real beauty. However, since they add little to the basic style or content which has already been discussed, there seems no reason for considering each of them in detail.

During the last decades of the Southern Sung dynasty there emerged yet another school of landscape painting which, under the impact of Ch'an Buddhism, produced some of the most original of Chinese paintings. Ch'an (Zen in Japanese) was a sect of Buddhism going back to the Indian Dhyani or meditation school. It is a branch which eliminates all dogma, all formal philosophy, and all traditional doctrine, teaching instead that the believer must devote himself entirely to meditation, for only when he is able to hear the inner voice in the depths of his consciousness will he understand the

truth which is Buddha. The members of this sect are close to the mystics
of other periods and other religions, for they preach that it is not by the
study of sacred writings that the believer finds union with the ultimate but
by a merging of the individual self into the soul pervading the cosmos. It
is typical that one of the most celebrated paintings of this school, which
was done by the famous Ch'an artist Liang K'ai, shows a patriarch of the
sect tearing up the sacred sutras to show that they are of no value in gaining
insight into ultimate reality.[72]

Liang K'ai, although primarily a painter of figures, did an occasional
landscape, such as the beautiful winter scene in the National Museum in
Tokyo.[73] The style is coarse by the standards of the Sung academicians, yet
it is this very quality which gives it boldness and force. The mood of winter,
with two solitary figures against the bleak landscape, is skillfully conveyed,
and the brushwork shows the strength of Liang K'ai's style.

Of the Ch'an landscape painters the most remarkable is Ying Yü-chien,
a monk living in the hills above the West Lake in the neighborhood of
Hang-chou, the Southern capital. Little is known about his life or career,
but several sections have come down to us of a magnificent scroll of the eight
views of the Hsiao and Hsiang Rivers. It was originally part of Yoshimasa's
collection, and it was later cut up by him so that he could enjoy all the views
at once by framing them. Today, some of these have disappeared, but others
are still in Japanese collections.[74] The most beautiful is undoubtedly the
one of a mountain village in the fog, formerly in the Matsudaira collection
and now in the Yoshikawa collection in Tokyo (Plate 45). Here the
technique of painting known as the "splashed-ink," or p'o mo, style is
brilliantly employed. There are no longer individual lines or definite areas
of ink; instead, the artist uses a stroke so free that it seems literally splashed
upon the paper. In this way the style has a certain similarity to that of
some modern Western artists, and there is no doubt that men like John
Marin were profoundly influenced not only by Chinese painting in general
but by this artist in particular. Naturally, such a style demands the utmost
concentration, for no mistake once made can be eliminated, no stroke put
down can be changed. The technique is closely related to Ch'an teaching,
for meditative Buddhism believes that the Buddha himself received ultimate

enlightenment by such a momentary flash of inspiration. So the artist should never attempt to work out his problems in a slow, systematic way, but he should wait for the moment when, seized by inspiration, a masterpiece can be created with a few rapid strokes. In this painting, Ying Yü-chien has scored a brilliant success, and all the familiar elements of the landscape—the bridge, trees, figures, buildings, and mountains—are fired with new and dynamic life. The reduction of forms to their essentials is carried to its extreme: one step further and the painting would be an abstraction. Little else in Chinese art is so intensely inspired, and with this work the last great attainment of the Southern Sung period had been achieved.

Another artist who worked in a similar though less extreme manner was Mu-ch'i, a Ch'an Buddhist monk whose fame in Japan is extremely great, while he is almost forgotten in his own country. His landscapes are very simple, without unnecessary detail or ornamental effect, and the result might well be considered a kind of shorthand by which his visions were translated into pictorial terms. Of his landscapes, the finest is the scroll of the eight views of the Hsiao and Hsiang Rivers *(Plate 46);* unfortunately it also has been cut up, and the various parts are now in Japanese collections.[75] The section reproduced here is a perfect illustration of his style, for it shows the soft, muted manner which is characteristic of the artist. The brush strokes are sometimes so delicate that they are barely visible, yet with this subtle and suggestive means the artist creates telling effects. Although he is similar in manner to Ying Yü-chien, Mu-ch'i lacks the vigor and boldness of the other artist, and one might say that his real stature lies somewhere between the excessive prestige he enjoys in Japan and the neglect which he suffers from his own countrymen.

With the Ch'an school this phase of landscape painting came to an end, and completely new ideals and new styles were developed in the following periods. One may or may not agree with the verdict of most Western scholars that the greatest epoch of Chinese painting had come to a close, but one can hardly doubt that the Southern Sung period was among the most creative in Chinese art and that the masterpieces of men such as Ma Yüan and Hsia Kuei have few if any equals in the history of painting.

58

7

The Yüan Period

A profound change in the landscape occurred during the fourteenth century under the Yüan dynasty, though it was neither the conquest of China by the Mongols in 1279 nor their artistic patronage which had such decisive effects, for most of the outstanding painters withdrew from the court life of the capital, preferring to live and work in solitude in their retreats rather than serve the foreign dynasty. Unquestionably the development of Chinese art would have taken the same direction even if the native Sung dynasty had continued, for the revolution which occurred in the outlook of the Chinese painters was an artistic rather than a political one. The nature of this change can probably best be summarized by comparing it to the transformation which Western art underwent during the late nineteenth and early twentieth century, when Cézanne and the modern movement brought about a similar revolution; while the earlier periods had been interested in the ideas and sentiments connected with landscape painting, the later one had what is best described as a formalistic approach. The Southern Sung artist had been profoundly philosophical, always stressing man's insignificance in relation to the universe, and the T'ang painters had placed primary emphasis upon the figure, using the landscape chiefly as a setting for the human scene portrayed, but the Yüan artists' chief interest was in the landscape itself, with human figures either not occurring or playing only an incidental part. They were concerned, as Cézanne was, with the structure of nature, and to them the form became more significant than the content.

Chinese critics and artists, especially during the Ch'ing period and again in modern times, have greatly admired the work of these painters and have regarded them as equal if not superior to those of the Sung period. The exponents of the Southern School saw in them their ideal of the gentleman-painter, for they were not professional artists working for money; they were amateurs who never belonged to the Academy or painted for the court, hermits and wanderers who lived the free life of the so-called *shan-jên* or *tao-jên*. Their lives were wholly dedicated to art and nature, and they lived far from the turmoil of the capital. Some of them, like the well-known Huang Kung-wang, became Taoists; others were Confucians; and all were educated men who were steeped in the classics and drew upon the main streams of Chinese thought.

Western critics have, for a long time, slighted the work of these painters, seeing it largely as an aftermath of the Sung period. Recently, however, their work has been re-evaluated, and now a number of scholars recognize it as a break with tradition.[76] How deep the change in the cultural ideals was is perhaps best illustrated by a quotation from the fourteenth-century painter and critic Wang Li:

The highest spirit and beauty can never be seized with the implements of painting. However, from that moment I advanced very quickly. I now know my own rules and do not trifle and follow in the dust of others. Every time I sit down in the empty hall with a peaceful mind looking in silence at the picture, the idea rises again—but this cannot be explained in words. How do I dare turn my back on my predecessors? But how can I help remaining outside the tradition established by them? It is common to find pleasure in that which is alike to oneself and not to rejoice in that which is different.—I kept the picture in my home and someone who happened to see it thought that it was contrary to every kind of style. Much surprised he asked me who my master was? To which I answered: I learned from my heart, my heart learned from my eye, and my eye from the Hua Mountains.[77]

The most distinguished of the Yüan landscape artists, and to the Chinese one of their greatest painters, was Huang Kung-wang. He was born in 1269 and died in 1354; so the main part of his artistic activity fell into the first half of the fourteenth century, the most creative part of the Yüan period.

Like many of these artists, he lived the life of a hermit and called himself the "Big Fool," or *Ta-ch'ih*, a typical Taoist name, and he wandered about the Fu-ch'un mountains, to which he had retired. There he observed the changing moods of nature, and unlike the artists of earlier periods, Huang Kung-wang (as well as some of his contemporaries) often worked in front of the very scene he was painting.

A typical work of his is the hanging scroll of his beloved Fu-ch'un mountains in the collection of Mr. P'ang Lai-chên in Shanghai *(Plate 47)*. At first, the theme may look similar to that of earlier paintings, but then it becomes clear that both in mood and style it is very different from anything in the Sung or the T'ang period. There is nothing philosophical about the painting—no sage gazing at the moon, no solitary traveller or lonely fisherman —nor is the work one of the splendid, elaborately-detailed scenes so typical of the T'ang period. Instead, the emphasis is upon structure, and the artist breaks the mountains up into groups of massive stone and sees the road as a series of diagonal thrusts. Buildings appear as little blocks, and the bridge at the right is used not as a bridge but as one of the formal elements of the composition. There are no figures, as is so often the case in Yüan painting, for the artist is no longer concerned either with human activity or man's position in nature.

The style of such paintings is very different from that of the Sung period, for the Yüan artists work more with areas of light and dark than with calligraphic lines. In the scene by Huang Kung-wang, these areas are used one against the other, creating a sense of atmosphere and space, though without the feeling of the infinitely-receding depth so characteristic of Sung painting. The pines appear as masses of foliage, sometimes completely dense and sometimes cut by white stems sharply dividing the dark areas. There is no emphasis upon twisting trunks and branches, no suggestion of picturesque shapes, either in the trees or in the mountains, whose simple, heavy forms have none of the wrinkles so prominent in earlier painting.

The large mountain landscape in the collection of Mr. Mathias Komor in New York is, according to its inscription, by Huang Kung-wang *(Plate 48)*. Although undoubtedly from the Yüan period, it seems closer in style to yet another painter, Wang Mêng, for it has the cubistic rocks and the flat

61

mountain peaks as well as the emphasis upon the outlines of the shapes with shading filled in later, a technique that the Chinese call *p'o mo,* or "broken-ink," which is characteristic of the style of Wang Mêng.[78] Whoever the artist may have been (and perhaps it was a third painter indebted to both), the work is typical of the period in its emphasis upon structural form. In this way, it is close to the modern art of the West, for it has the same concern with the abstract at the expense of illusionistic appearance or narrative content. It is most instructive to compare this painting with two other treatments of the same theme: the T'ang "Travellers in Mountain Landscape" in Peking and the Sung "Tribute Horse" in the Metropolitan. In the first, the figures dominate the scene, and every detail is exactly drawn with hard contours and bright colors. The emphasis in the second has passed from the figures to the mountains, with both outlines and colors less pronounced, while in the Yüan work the figures are hardly apparent and certainly not essential, and the brush strokes are free, with only light touches of color added to the basic monochrome.

A work which can be positively identified as one by Wang Mêng, a painter who lived from around 1308 to 1385, is the landscape scroll in the Freer *(Plate 49).* Here one sees the same concern for form, particularly in the rocks, whose fantastic shapes, so similar to the sculptures of the modern English artist Henry Moore, are more important than the house or the figures. Of equal concern was the artist's skill in using his brush, and once this formal approach is understood, the painting of the Yüan dynasty assumes a character of its own and can no longer be considered as a late phase of Sung or, as it has sometimes been called, a period of transition.

The Yüan painter who is probably the best known and most admired in the West is Ni Tsan, who lived from 1301 to 1374. He too was a hermit who had withdrawn from official life, and he is famous for his sensitive views of autumn, which express in a very moving way the loneliness and melancholy of the season. Since he was much admired, many later artists either copied him or worked in his manner, so that one sees numerous paintings which resemble his, both in style and motif.

A typical work, the "Autumn Landscape" scroll in the Freer Gallery in Washington, shows his characteristic theme rendered with the utmost delicacy *(Plate 50)*. The technique he employs is known as *kan pi,* or "dry-brush painting," a method in which the artist, by taking very little ink, is able to achieve the subtle, sketchy stroke which Ni Tsan uses in this painting. The composition is very simple, with trees forming a vertical at the right and the diagonal of the trunk leading to the band of mountains which move out horizontally from the left. In the foreground there are a few rocks, a pavilion, and then the lake in the middle suggested largely by the paper. Every stroke is meaningful, and the effect of these simple forms is to create a mood, quiet and restrained, which conveys a sense of autumn.

Another Yüan scroll in the Freer Gallery, one which has a similar delicacy, is the "Interminable Rivers and Mountains" scroll by Hsü Pên, of the late fourteenth century *(Plate 51)*. This particular painting, since it was done in 1377, already falls into the Ming period, but it shows that this same style which we associate with the Yüan period continued during most of the fourteenth century, even after the native Ming dynasty had assumed power in 1368. Although the "dry-brush manner" is not quite as noticeable here as in the Ni Tsan, there is the same tendency to use a minimum of ink, and the result is a stroke both light and graceful, which gives the work a beauty of its own.

The subject is again the mountains, the winding river, the waterfall, the trees and houses, and tiny figures, a theme treated innumerable times by Kuo Hsi and the Northern Sung painters. However, both the spirit in which the landscape is approached and the style of the painting are very different, and even here, where there are many figures, and mist lies in the valley or obscures a ridge, the real emphasis is still upon form. If one looks at the painting from a distance, the details disappear, and what stands out is the structure of the mountains, bony and furrowed and very strong in spite of the delicate brush.

Another Yüan painter, Kao K'o-kung, represents a somewhat different tendency in the painting of his time. He was the earliest of the three great Yüan artists, and unlike the others, he served under Kublai Khan. In some ways he is closer to the Sung tradition, and his work, which is modelled upon Mi Fei's, bears a striking resemblance to that of the Northern Sung painter, especially in the use of the "splashed-ink" technique. His style is

63

very spontaneous, and we are told that "under the influence of wine, or in the company of good friends, he would seize silk or paper and flourish the brush, and then, in the exhilaration of the moment he would throw off astounding sketches, as though his hand were guided by some spiritual power."[79]

A typical painting is the scroll entitled "Rain in the Mountains" in the Detroit Art Institute, which is dated 1308 *(Plate 52)*. In contrast to the works of Mi Fei, this lacks subtlety both in mood and brushwork, but it is powerful in its bold use of ink washes, its strong contrasts of light and dark, and its expressive rendering of the rain-swept scene. There are many such landscapes ascribed to Kao K'o-kung, some of them undoubtedly copies or paintings done by later artists working in his manner, yet all of them exhibit the same characteristic style.

The few works discussed here are only a small part of the numerous Yüan paintings which have survived, for with this period our knowledge becomes more definite, and a large number of originals are available, especially in Chinese collections. Under these circumstances it is impossible to do more than indicate the spirit and dominant style, for only a book far more ambitious could consider all the artists and paintings. Even from this brief study, however, it is apparent that the painting of the Yüan dynasty has a character of its own and that, far from imitating the work of the Sung period, artists like Huang Kung-wang developed a kind of painting which, with its emphasis upon form, represented a completely new approach to the art of the landscape.

8

The Ming Period

WITH the advent of the native dynasty, especially after the Ming rulers in 1409 once again moved the capital to Peking, there was a fresh outburst of artistic creativity. Again the painting changed, and although the landscape was no longer as important as it had been during Sung times it expressed the new ideals of the period, which was both rational and materialistic. Ming painting, although often artistically rewarding, lacks the depths of feeling and profundity of thought which had characterized the best of Sung painting. The center is again man, and in this way the Ming period seems closer to the T'ang than to the periods which immediately preceded it. Human activities are shown as interesting in themselves, and there is a strong anecdotal tendency in much of the painting, which is now concerned, not with man's place in the universe, but with his life in the daily world. Hand in hand with this goes another development—that of a greater emphasis upon realistic detail. It was not that most Ming artists used the meticulous style so characteristic of T'ang painting, but that they were more interested in describing the details of a given scene, while earlier painters, such as Ma Yüan or Ni Tsan, had been satsified with subtle suggestion.

Despite these changes, respect for tradition was still strong, and the Ming artists at least professed to be following the masters of previous dynasties. Many a work shows the influence of the great Southern Sung academicians

Hsia Kuei and Ma Yüan, while others reflect the Yüan masters or return to painters of the Northern Sung period such as Tung Yüan, Chü-jan, Kuo Hsi, and Mi Fei. However, the most creative artists show a style distinctly different from any in the earlier periods, a style which expresses the cultural and social forces of this age, when the Chinese, under the native house of Ming, enjoyed tremendous power and prosperity. Chinese critics, always intent upon emphasizing the traditional and, at the same time, dedicated to the concept of the two conflicting schools, the Southern and the Northern, have failed to emphasize the unique character of the age, and Western critics until very recently have tended to neglect the period altogether.

Most Chinese critics, with their characteristic love of classification, have divided Ming art into two opposing schools: the Wu School named after Wu-hsien, a part of modern Suchou, and the Chê School after Chêkiang province, because the leading artists of the respective groups came from these places. The members of the former were looked upon as descendents of the Southern School since they also were gentlemen-painters, while those of the latter, who were mostly professional artists, were linked to the Northern School. This division, which has been discussed earlier, became far more important during the Ming period, when such leading critics as Tung Ch'i-ch'ang viewed all Chinese painting in the light of these two traditions. The tendency on his part as well as that of other critics was to praise the artists of the Southern School for being the true exponents of the *wên jên hua,* the painting of the literati, because they were amateurs who neither painted for a living nor served as court artists. Those who were at the court had positions as officials or scholars, while others lived as hermits, and still others were gentlemen who created only for their own pleasure, giving their pictures away instead of selling them. They were usually educated men—scholars, writers, poets, and calligraphers—in addition to being artists, and often, especially in the case of Tung Ch'i-ch'ang, their fame rested more upon their standing in these fields than upon their excellence as painters. Actually, this strict division means very little when one studies the work of these artists, for the same tendencies characteristic of the Ming period may be seen in the members of each school, and many painters, especially those of the sixteenth century, show elements of both, so that it becomes impossible

66

to classify them in one camp or the other. A close parallel may be seen in our own use of the terms classic and romantic, or romantic and realistic, concepts which in a pure sense may be deeply meaningful but when applied to particular artists tend to lose their clarity, for aspects of both may be found in the work of a single artist or even a single painting, and a man who starts out with one school may end up with another, so that a strict classification is often more confusing than helpful.

The leading master of the Wu School and one of the greatest Ming painters was Shên Chou, who lived from 1427 to 1509. He is usually referred to as the founder of this school, and he was much esteemed not only for his inspired art but also for his hermit's life, worthy of a *wên jên* to whom painting was one of the ornaments of the educated man. He was said to continue in the great traditions of Chinese painting, going back to Wang Wei, the so-called founder of the Southern School, and to be particularly influenced by the Yüan masters, especially Wu Chên, whose broad, spontaneous brushwork resembles his own. In spite of all this, Shên Chou is an artist of originality, and his work is basically different from that of the preceding painters.

This difference is apparent in the river landscape in the Freer Gallery, a typical Shên Chou painting *(Plate 53)*. Unlike the river scenes of the Sung or the Yüan periods, this is a genre painting in which the artist records the life of the river. There are dozens of figures, some fishing, some picnicking, others strolling or resting; but all concern themselves with daily pursuits, and they are too absorbed in their own affairs to be interested in the beauty of the setting. The houses are not mountain retreats, but a group of dwellings where the fishermen live; and the rocks and trees have no significance in themselves, but are painted as part of the scenery. The brushwork is very loose, and the ink is applied with broad and sometimes heavy strokes, which give a strength to the painting very different from the delicacy so typical of a Yüan artist like Ni Tsan.

Another work by Shên Chou is the picture called "Poet on a Mountain," which forms part of a longer scroll consisting of six panels *(Plates 54 and 55)*. Here it would seem as though Shên Chou had returned to the kind of motif popular during the Sung period, but neither the spirit nor the

67

execution of the painting resembles the Sung scrolls. Far from creating a misty depth or emphasizing aerial perspective, the space is rather shallow, and the mountain on which the poet stands is rendered in broad, heavy strokes. The peaks to the left and right have no modelling at all, and the almost expressionistic use of the ink, particularly in the section showing the house between the trees, is very powerful, with its strong contrasts of light and dark, though it lacks the subtle beauty of the Sung masters.

The outstanding painter of the Chê School was Tai Chin, probably a contemporary of Shên Chou, although he must have died long before the other. He was called to court, but apparently, due to the jealousy of other painters, he did not find the favor he had expected and was forced to return to his native province, where he died, neglected and poor. However, his genius was so great that, despite his lack of success and the hostility of the critics, his fame continued to grow, and his position as the leading painter of the Chê School is undisputed. According to contemporary accounts, he followed the masters of the Sung period, especially Ma Yüan and Li T'ang, and there are works of his which show the influence of these painters, but his mature style is very independent. Like all artists, he undoubtedly drew upon the discoveries of earlier periods, but, original as he was, he transformed these influences into something uniquely his own.

The two river-scene scrolls in the Freer Gallery are the best of his surviving works and, for that matter, are among the finest paintings of the period. Chinese critics always placed a great emphasis upon the difference between Tai Chin and Shên Chou, and when one considers this, it is surprising to see that Tai Chin's paintings, especially the scroll called "Autumn River Landscape with Fishing Boats," are really quite similar to the river scene of Shên Chou (*Plates 56 and 57*). There are the same sharp contrasts of ink tones and the same broad and full brush as well as the emphasis upon narrative, with the life of the fishermen creating a busy, animated scene. The treatment of the space is likewise similar to that of Shên Chou, for the action occurs mostly in the foreground, with little feeling of depth and none of the mist half hiding and half revealing the mountains, which had been such a beloved motif of the Southern Sung artists whom Tai Chin is supposed to have followed. Above all, there is a strength of brushwork and a power of tonal effect, in this case reinforced by some color, and in each a design which is both original and expressive.

The other "River Landscape" in the Freer Gallery is considered by some critics to be superior to the one discussed above *(Plates 58 and 59)*. The subject is very similar, although there is less emphasis upon the trees and grass, and the river is shown in a storm, with boats rocking on the waves and trees bending, while the weather in the first was calm and sunny. In keeping with the greater drama, Tai Chin uses stronger contrasts between dark and light, setting the black mass of the shore next to the white of the paper, on which waves are indicated by undulating lines. Again, the scene is very vivid, and we see the struggle of the boatsmen as they work against the wind, and the alarm of some of the passengers who peer out from the cabins. On the hill there is a man riding a donkey, his shoulders hunched about his head, and behind a servant comes carrying a large umbrella. Each detail, no matter how vivid, takes its place in the design, and the whole is painted with the freedom and simplicity which marks a work of genius.

The two leading artists of the early sixteenth century were Wên Chêng-ming and T'ang Yin, who were both born in 1470, although the first lived until 1559, while the second, after a wild and carefree life, died in 1524. Chinese tradition puts both in the Wu School, especially Wên Chêng-ming, who was a pupil of Shên Chou. However, they are quite original in their style, which was created from many influences, particularly that of Li T'ang, whom they are supposed to have studied assiduously. While Shên Chou had been a hermit, these sixteenth-century masters were more worldly, Wên Chêng-ming being a scholar and gentleman, while T'ang Yin, who loved a gay life, was well known for his drinking and amorousness.

A typical work by Wên Chêng-ming is the landscape in the Freer Gallery, which is dated 1536 *(Plate 60)*. It shows a beautiful river scene with rocks and trees and a pavilion where two gentlemen are engaged in conversation. The theme is traditional, yet it is treated in a characteristic Ming manner, with heavy blacks set against lighter tones, a loose application of ink, and a shallow space. The brushwork is very strong, especially in the rocks and the shadowed areas of the trees, and its boldness gives the painting a certain originality. Other works of his differ considerably, for it appears that during

69

his long life Wên Chêng-ming used various styles. However, it is this type of painting which shows him at his best, and it may be added that in such work he seems as indebted to Tai Chin as he was to his teacher, Shên Chou.

T'ang Yin's style is more meticulous, and in spite of belonging to the Wu School, he seems closer in spirit to the painters of the Southern Sung Academy and to the tradition associated with the Chê School. Here again, the finest example of his work, a landscape scroll, is found in the Freer Gallery *(Plate 61)*. The motif of the mountains, the gnarled pines, and the scholar alone in his retreat is certainly typical of the Southern Sung period, as is the greater emphasis upon depth and the misty ridges in the background. At the same time it is unmistakably from the Ming period, since it has far more detail and shows a greater contrast between light and dark areas. The result is a work of decorative beauty, but it has neither the expressive power of painters like Tai Chin, nor the profundity and lyricism of Ma Yüan and Hsia Kuei.

Somewhat younger than these two artists and very different in style was Ch'iu Ying, who, although not very celebrated in his own time, has since become famous. As he was a typical exponent of the Northern School and neither a poet nor a scholar, the Chinese writers did not consider his career of great enough interest to record it. As a result, little is known about his life, but it is believed that his main artistic activity occurred between 1522 and 1560. A great number of works are ascribed to him, and although he was a prolific painter, it seems probable that the bulk of them are copies or, even more likely, works executed in the manner traditionally associated with his name, a style marked by careful detail and bright colors similar to that of the outstanding exponents of the Northern School like Li Ssu-hsün and Chao Po-chü.

Among the many works attributed to him, probably the most charming is the one in the collection of the Chion-in in Kyoto *(Plate 62)*. Here, describing a garden feast where poets are entertained by graceful girls, the artist is at his best, an engaging painter who enjoys celebrating the pleasures of man. His view of nature is an intimate one, and the pines and rocks and flowering trees are used to enhance the charm of the setting. As a genre painting it is typical of the period, and in spite of the difference in subject and style it is closely related to the works of the other Ming artists we have considered. Its manner is exquisitely detailed, especially in the figures, each so carefully finished, and in the trees, where every twig and flower is drawn with delicate precision. The ink is applied more sparingly than in the work of the great fifteenth-century painters, and the bright colors reinforce the decorative pattern of the whole. This type of painting, although slighted by the critics of the literary school, was immensely popular with the Chinese people and had a tremendous influence, especially during the eighteenth century, when a narrative and decorative style was widely used. It was also painting like this which first aroused enthusiasm for Chinese art in Europe, and it might be said that for several centuries Europeans identified Chinese painting with such decorative work.

The most creative period of Ming art came to a close with the death of Wên Chêng-ming and Ch'iu Ying. It had run parallel with the Renaissance in Europe, lasting through the fifteenth century and the first half of the sixteenth, and during the next century there was little of interest. The dominant artistic figures were men such as Tung Ch'i-ch'ang, who was more outstanding as a critic and scholar than as a creative artist. These men were academicians in the worst sense of the word, men who looked only to the past for inspiration and discouraged any original tendencies. The result was a lifeless art in which every stroke was prescribed and no departure from tradition was tolerated. They believed that if the artist combined the best points from each of the painters of the past, he would produce a perfect picture, yet the result, as may be well imagined, was the very opposite. Like all such art, it failed, for in spite of the rules and the manuals, it lacked the life which had inspired the masterpieces of earlier times.

The theory of eclecticism which characterized the late Ming period is perfectly expressed in a quotation from Tung Ch'i-ch'ang, the spokesman of the academic school:

In calligraphy it is possible to create new styles: but in painting the familiar is essential. In calligraphy a man may start with the familiar and go on to the experimental; but in painting he must begin and end with the familiar. In painting distances one should imitate Chao Ta-nien; in mountains and crags piled one above the other, Chiang Kuan-tao should be the model. For outline use, Tung Yüan's hemp skin method or the dotted style of Hsiao Hsiang views. For three-outline, go to

71

Tung Yüan and Mêng-fu. As Li Ch'êng sometimes painted in opaque greens and blues as well as in ink, he may be copied in all styles. . . . It has been said that in tree painting one is free to make one's own style. Nothing could be more untrue! For willow trees Chao Po-chü is the standard; for pines Ma Ho-chih; for withered trees Li Ch'êng. These laws are of great antiquity and cannot be changed. Slight modifications may of course be introduced, provided they do not impinge on the essentials. How absurd to speak of abandoning the old method and creating a new! . . . The prime essential is that the painter should imitate the Old Masters. After that he may go on to the imitation of natural objects.[80]

The result of this teaching, which unfortunately was widely accepted, was a marked decline in painting during the last part of the Ming period, and it was not until the middle of the seventeenth century that new currents in art arose.

9

The Ch'ing Period

BEGINNING with the Manchu dynasty in 1644 there was in the arts a renewed period of vigorous activity, especially under K'ang Hsi (1662—1722) and his grandson, Ch'ien Lung (1736—1795), who were among the most active patrons of the arts that China has ever known. It was during these years that the famous *Imperial Encyclopedia of Calligraphy and Painting,* the *Ch'in Ting P'ei Wên Chai Shu Hua P'u,* was issued in one hundred volumes. As far as the artistic merit of this tremendous output is concerned, there is a great difference in scholarly opinion. The Chinese themselves have considered the outstanding artists of the early Ch'ing period, especially the four Wangs, as among the greatest of Chinese painters, while most Western critics have for a long time tended to dismiss the entire artistic output as too eclectic to be of interest. Only in recent years have Western scholars devoted their attention to this vast field and begun to take a more positive attitude towards the art of the Manchu dynasty.[81] The truth probably lies somewhere between the two positions, for clearly the painting of the last three centuries cannot be compared with the great art of the preceding ages, yet, at the same time, Western critics, having trained themselves entirely by a study of the Southern Sung painters whose works first became available in the magnificent Japanese publications, could not appreciate the painting of the famous Ch'ing masters.

The emphasis during these years was completely upon tradition, and neither painters nor critics tired of reiterating the teachings of Tung Ch'i-ch'ang, who had first proclaimed that all good art followed the ancients, especially the masters of the T'ang, Sung, and Yüan dynasties. Among these, the most famous during the Ch'ing period were Wang Wei, Li Ch'êng, Tung Yüan, Chü-jan, Fan K'uan, Huang Kung-wang, Ni Tsan, Wu Chên, and Wang Mêng, all of whose works were copied or imitated over and over again. In fact, the bulk of the artistic output of these years was inspired by the painters of the past. Nevertheless, it is striking how the work of this age has a character which cannot be confused with that of the Sung or Yüan periods. The same artist can produce pictures in the style of a great many earlier painters (whose works he may or may not have been familiar with), yet they tend to look so alike that it is often impossible to tell which was inspired by Tung Yüan and which by Huang Kung-wang, so great is the similarity.

Of the four best-known academic painters, the greatest in the eyes of his own and later periods was Wang Hui, who lived from 1632 to 1717. The others were Wang Shih-min, Wang Chien, and Wang Yüan-ch'i, and the group was therefore known as the "Four Wangs." Wang Hui was above all a tremendous virtuoso, a man of great skill and inventiveness, but since he was without originality he was an eclectic in the true sense of the word. His knowledge of the old masters was immense, and he tried to adapt the best from each, but he made no contribution of his own.

A typical painting, one in the Freer Gallery, is the landscape scroll representing Mount Fu-ch'un (*Plates 63 and 64*), which characteristically enough is inspired by a work like the famous Huang Kung-wang scroll of the same site in the Palace Museum in Peking.[82] Like the Yüan artist, Wang Hui is primarily interested in the formal structure of the mountains, rocks, and trees, and in the quality of the brushwork rather than in any philosophical meaning or narrative content. Yet, when compared with the earlier painting, the result is thin and uninspired, for it lacks the very quality which Hsieh Ho, the fifth-century critic, was referring to when he said that the artist should possess above all the *ch'i yün,* or "life spirit." Lacking this, the trees are not alive, nor does the water flow or the space have depths, and the mountains show little real feeling of mass. The individual strokes may well reveal, as the Chinese critics maintain, a remarkable skill in handling the brush, but the total effect is disappointing when one considers the fame of the artist.

While the painters who gave expression to the ideals of the critics completely dominated the official scene, there were other artists who, far from the glamour of the court life of the capital, created very different kinds of painting. They were mostly Taoist monks who lived withdrawn from the world and paid little attention to the traditionalists, and they were not appreciated by the Confucian society of the day. It is perhaps only in very recent times that, both in the Far East as well as in the West, their highly original style has been accepted. It may well be that the growth of modern abstract painting helped bring about their recognition, for they were also "Fauves," wild men who rebelled against tradition and were accused by their contemporaries of being uncouth, though later generations saw them as being among the most outstanding artists of their age.

The most famous is Tao-chi, better known as Shih-t'ao, who was born in 1630 and died in 1707 and was therefore an almost exact contemporary of Wang Hui. He is well known not only for his painting but also for an essay entitled *Hua Yü Lu*.[83] This most extraordinary document is a discussion of painting couched in brilliant but often obscure images derived from both Taoist and Confucian sources. The author's basic ideas are the very opposite of those then prevailing, for he believed that the artist should, above all, be guided by his own inspiration and that "the method which consists in following no method is the perfect method." To him genius and inspiration were the main things, and knowledge was secondary.

His painting style, as one might expect, is spontaneous and though sometimes crude, often very expressive. He follows the spirit of the Yüan artists insofar as he is primarily a formalist to whom the quality of the brushwork is all-important and the subject matter secondary. A characteristic painting of his, an album leaf in a private Chinese collection, shows the strength of his brushwork which, especially in the broad, dark strokes of the mountain and in the loosely-indicated trees, is very powerful *(Plate 65)*. A solitary black peak stands dramatically against a light sky, and smaller, more distant mountains are rendered in subtle, simply-painted half tones. The foreground is wonderfully free, resembling in its spontaneous style the modern Expressionists of the Western world, who also believe in following their own inspiration. Nevertheless, in spite of the difference between the temperaments and philosophies of the traditional Wang Hui and the eccentric Shih-t'ao, their basic approach is surprisingly similar. Both of them are, above all, formalists whose chief concern is with the quality of the strokes and the underlying structure of nature rather than with philosophical or narrative painting, and in this way they are an expression of their age despite their apparent opposition.

Another artist belonging to the same group and carrying this inspired and spontaneous style of painting to even greater extremes is the monk Chu Ta, better known as Pa-ta Shan-jên, who lived from 1626 to about 1705. His scroll of "Rocks and Fish" in a New York private collection is typical of the abstract quality of his style *(Plate 66)*. In it the brush stroke has assumed a meaning in itself, almost completely divorced from the subject matter, which, as in much modern painting in the West, is no longer very important, for the artist is concerned with the expressiveness of the sweeping lines and the abstract shapes. The result is often very forceful; yet, striking as it is, it lacks the depths of the great painting of the past.

With the eighteenth and nineteenth centuries, the prevailing eclecticism became even more pronounced, and little new was contributed to the development of landscape painting. Nevertheless, the skill of the artists continued, and they produced pictures which are often very pleasant. It is impossible even to attempt a survey of these many and diverse artistic personalities, for the closer we come to our own time, the greater is the number of originals which have survived. However, two examples may give some idea of what the paintings of the Southern and the Northern Schools of this age were like.

A typical product of the Southern School is the Yüan Chiang painting dated 1754 and entitled "Carts on a Winding Mountain Road" in the collection of the Nelson Gallery in Kansas City *(Plate 67)*. According to the inscription, it was inspired by the work of Kuo Hsi, and the theme of the mountains towering over the pines and over the tiny figures on the bridge and the road is typical of the Northern Sung artist. But there the resemblance ends, for

76

the style, with its painstaking detail, is labored and dry. There is a wealth of minutiae; yet despite the exquisiteness of even the tiniest parts the details do not come together. The mountain in particular falls into separate pieces, and the whole, though it has a certain charm, fails to be convincing.

An excellent example of the more colorful Northern School of painting is the famous scroll of "Sages in a Landscape" in the collection of the Freer Gallery (Plate 68). Since its style, with its use of brilliant color and gold outlines, was associated with the famous T'ang painter Li Ssu-hsün, it was once attributed to him, but today it is no longer regarded as even a copy of his work, but as an eighteenth-century painting done in a manner reminiscent of the T'ang tradition. Nevertheless, it is an extremely pleasant painting, and its hard clarity gives it a charm of its own. The brushwork is very skillful, and the motif of the sages wandering about in the landscape is characteristic of this type of painting.

The tendency towards imitation and the emphasis upon tradition was equally strong in the nineteenth century, and a landscape by Wang Cheng-kuo, dated 1812 and in the collection of Mr. Mathias Komor, illustrates the trend (Plate 69). It is done in the style of Wang Hui, who continued to enjoy a tremendous reputation, and it shows the traditional theme of the sage in the mountain landscape. The skill of the artist is considerable, but he was not able to infuse the painting with any vigor, and its deadness is an indication that, by this time, the art of the landscape had lost all creative life.

In the twentieth century the landscape has continued to be the most beloved of all subjects in Chinese painting, and both the traditional and the Western-orientated painters have gone on producing landscapes in great numbers. Here again it would be impossible to give an adequate idea of the various artists at work, many of whom are really more Western than Chinese, but the "Rocks and Water" scroll of Wang Chi-ch'üan, a contemporary painter now living in the United States, may give some idea of how the modern artist brings fresh life to the traditional subject (Plate 70). Perhaps the use of various planes in rendering space shows a knowledge of Western perspective, but otherwise it is a typical Chinese landscape painted with a loose brush and strongly contrasting ink tones. As in the work of

Shih-t'ao, the emphasis is upon the expressive power of the strokes rather than the poetic mood or the illustrative content, and the result is a vigorous and fine work of art.

With the victory of the Communist regime, the great and ancient tradition of landscape painting has, at least for the time being, come to an end on the Chinese mainland. The new masters of the Middle Kingdom are Marxists who have little sympathy for Taoist inspiration or literary painting; instead, they sponsor a Western-style art which is political in character. Man stands in the center, although now as an instrument of an all-powerful police state, and it is to the glorification of man's social and political achievements that art is dedicated. Naturally, there is no longer a place for the free artist in such a society, and, like the earlier painters who fled when barbaric rulers took over, many of the most gifted Chinese artists have gone into exile.

The Landscape Painting
of
JAPAN

10

The Beginnings of Landscape Painting in Japan

A love of nature has, from the earliest times, been one of the outstanding characteristics of the Japanese people. Their native religion is little more than a worship of the spirits of nature, for in Shintoism the whole of creation is believed to be inhabited by multitudes of *kami,* or gods. The greatest of these was the Sun Goddess, whose shrine at Ise is still one of the most venerated in Japan, but mountains and rivers, trees and flowers, earth and stones were all thought to have their spirits. This belief in an animate world was certainly one of the factors in the development of the love of nature, and another was the beauty of the islands, which for centuries painters and poets have celebrated in their art. The *Manyōshū*, the famous collection of poetry from the Nara period, contains a number of lyrics which express the deep intimacy between man and nature, one of which, written by Ōtomo Yakamochi in A.D. 747, is as follows:

> In the land of Koshi
> Famous among the distant regions,
> Many are the mountains
> And countless rivers run,

But on Mount Tachi of Niikawa
Because of its divinity,
Snow lies throughout summer.
Unlike the mists that form and lift
Each morning and evening
Over the limpid shallows
Of the engirdling Katakai,
The mountain will not leave our memory.
Each year I will come
And gaze upon the mountain afar,
Then speak of it to those
Yet strangers to its beauty,
Spreading its fame to future years,
That all who but hear its name
May long to see it.[84]

In many of these poems, there is a depth of feeling not equalled in the lyrics even of the contemporary Chinese poets. The following, written in 753, is one of the loveliest of the *Manyōshū* lyrics:

Over the spring field trails the mist,
And lonely is my heart;
Then in this fading light of evening
A warbler sings.
Through the little bamboo bush
Close to my chamber,
The wind blows faintly rustling
In this evening dusk.[85]

As in China, the rise of landscape painting came long after the development of nature poetry. In fact, before the introduction of Buddhism to Japan, there was no painting to speak of—only abstract, geometrical designs and primitive line drawings. However, after Japan entered the cultural orbit of the Chinese in the second half of the sixth century, the scene changed radically, and the Chinese influence was completely dominant during the seventh and eighth centuries. As has already been mentioned in the chapter on T'ang art, some of the most important of the early Chinese landscape paintings have been preserved in the Shōsō-in, and it is largely due to these monuments that we have been able to reconstruct a picture of T'ang painting. During the Nara period (710—794) the Chinese influence was so strong that it is often impossible to tell if a given work was executed by a Japanese artist, or by a Chinese working on the continent, or by a Chinese or a Korean artist working in Japan.

The earliest of these Japanese landscapes are painted on the Tamamushi Shrine, a miniature replica of a temple which is kept at Hōryū-ji. Although the exact date is not known, the stylistic affinities with the sculptures of the Sui period, especially in the treatment of the long, slender bodies, would indicate that the Chinese prototype was of the late sixth or the early seventh century. If one takes into consideration the cultural lag between China proper and the outlying areas, this would suggest a date about the middle of the seventh century, or the end of the Asuka period, for the Japanese work. The paintings, which are done on wood, represent Jataka scenes, or stories about the incarnations of the Buddha during which he performed meritorious deeds, and the religious figures completely dominate the setting.

The scene reproduced is typical of this kind of painting, where the landscape is reduced to a few abstract and highly simplified elements (*Plate 71*). The most prominent are the curiously stratified cliffs, the bamboo in the center, the tree at the upper right with birds on its branches, and the undulating hills with trees and tiny bushes. Since no contemporary Chinese paintings of this type have survived, it is impossible to tell what the relationship is between this work and its Chinese and Korean models, but the use of mountains and trees as the primary elements of the landscape is certainly characteristic of the Chinese paintings of this early period. The only detail which might suggest something typically Japanese is the treatment of the mountains which, with their rhythmic, swelling forms, seems to foreshadow the landscape paintings of the Heian and later periods. Thus it would appear that even at this early date the Japanese artist had begun to introduce elements which reflected his native environment. It may also be said that the style of these paintings is far more skillful than that of any contemporary works which have been preserved in China, yet in spite of this the landscape painting during this period was still extremely primitive, especially in its treatment of space and depth and the actual appearance of nature.

A work done at a somewhat later date, although probably based on an earlier original, is the *Kako Genzai Inga Kyō,* or the "Sutra of the Past and Present Karma," which portrays episodes from the life of Sakyamuni before he became an ascetic *(Plate 72)*. Originally there were eight scrolls, and the remnants, which are remarkably well preserved, are now scattered in various public and private Japanese collections. They are of great historical interest, both in themselves and in their foreshadowing of the rise of the native Japanese school of narrative scroll painting of the *e-makimono* variety. Tradition has it that the second scroll, now lost, bore a colophon with the date 735, and it is believed that Japanese artists copied a Chinese sutra of that period.[86] Although the calligraphy is of the T'ang type, the style of the painting is of an earlier date, with a landscape which is little more than a crude setting and figures recalling sixth-century carvings. For example, some of the tempters of Sakya in the portion of the set kept in the Hō-nin of the Daigo-ji in Kyoto[87] show, in the treatment of the garments, the same kind of angular, zigzag pattern which is found in early sixth-century Chinese bronzes or in Japanese works such as the *Yumedono Kannon*. The mountains and trees, on the other hand, are similar to those of the early sixth-century sarcophogi, although they are executed in a somewhat cruder style. This is not surprising, however, since Buddhist painting, as we have already seen at Tun Huang, appears to have lagged behind in its development. Certainly these scrolls would suggest that the landscape painting of the Buddhist sutras was still in its earliest stage, for despite the naïve charm of the painting, its treatment of space and of the natural elements is still very primitive. The colors are fresh and bright, and as in the Tamamushi paintings, the mountains and trees, which are rendered almost entirely by heavy contour lines, are the main elements of the setting.

The works in the Shōsō-in are of a very different and far more advanced style. This collection, which consists of some three thousand objects containing all the types of arts and crafts common in T'ang China and introduced from there to the Nara court, has been preserved in the storehouse of Tōdai-ji in Nara since 765 when, at the death of the Emperor Shōmu, his widow dedicated it to the famous temple. It is a collection of unique value, for not only have the records of the treasures been preserved, but the objects themselves have been kept at the same place for the last twelve hundred years. The origin of many of these works is a matter of debate, with most Japanese scholars tending to consider them of Japanese manufacture,[88] while the late Dr. Kümmel, the leading German scholar in the field, believed them to be of Chinese origin.[89] Probably there is some truth in both positions, for no doubt many of the objects were either originally imported from China or sent to Japan as presents from the T'ang court, while others may well have been made in Japan by Chinese craftsmen or by native artisans imitating Chinese models. In any case there is no doubt that the works closely follow continental prototypes, since they are far in advance of any similar work produced in Japan either previously or in the generations which followed.

According to the original deed of gift still preserved at the Shōsō-in, the collection at one time included actual landscape paintings. For example, there was a pair of six-fold screens with landscapes, as well as a single six-fold screen with a landscape, in the ancient style, but none of these have survived.[90] However, there are several excellent landscapes, already mentioned in the discussion of T'ang painting, which reflect the T'ang style. Among them the landscapes on the mirrors, metal bowls, lacquer objects, textiles, and musical instruments are the most remarkable. The ones particularly revealing for this study are the two paintings on the plectrum guards of biwa's, a kind of Japanese lute; the landscape on a large hemp cloth; and the landscape painting in gold on the top of a wooden box.[91]

The most interesting of all is probably the picture on one of the biwa's of three musicians and a dancer riding an elephant, against a background of mountain scenery (Plate 73). Scholars have disagreed as to whether this is a Chinese painting or a Japanese one following Chinese models, but there can be no doubt that it is a close reflection of the T'ang painting of the eighth century. Even if it is Chinese (as seems likely), it is the work of an artisan rather than of one of the great court painters, yet since it is of unquestioned authenticity, it gives us something solid to build upon. If one compares it with the "Travellers in Mountain Landscape" in the Peking Palace Museum, one finds a striking affinity between the two paintings. In both there are prominent figures worked out in great detail, and mountains, rising sharply and crested with trees, are modelled in light and dark. Each has a vista opening into the background, with a series of hills which draws the eye into space, and in both there are bright colors in contrast to the monochrome which

85

prevailed later. In spite of a marked advance in the rendering of space, the transition from fore- to background is still awkward in both paintings, with little feeling for either atmosphere or the natural appearance of the landscape.

Another work of great interest is the highly abstract landscape on hemp showing a lake with islands, trees, rocks, grasses, and a single figure with a fishing pole *(Plate 74)*. The style is very simple with a few quick, sure lines brushed directly onto the rough surface, leaving the cloth to suggest the natural forms as well as the space. Though the means are simple, the effect is very remarkable, indicating an artist of considerable skill. It would seem likely that a painter who could do such a charming landscape on a rough piece of cloth could have painted highly-developed landscapes on silk or paper, and we can only lament the loss of all the contemporary scrolls, screens, and wall paintings showing landscapes, for undoubtedly there were many not only in China but also in Nara Japan.

Of the many other landscapes on the objects in the Shōsō-in, probably the most striking is the mountain landscape in gold on the lid of a box. With its freely-painted style and its mountains, pines, birds, and swirling clouds, it shows a high degree of sophistication, leaving no doubt that the artists who produced it were the product of a highly-developed school of landscape painters. Here again, the similarity between the steep mountains, with their many wrinkled layers, and those in the Peking landscape with travellers is very striking. Scholarly opinion seems more inclined to view this work as one which was actually executed in Japan, but even if this were the case there is no doubt that the style closely follows that of its Chinese models.

If one can judge from these relatively fragmentary remains, the Nara period must have had a varied and impressive output of landscape painting. The style undoubtedly mirrored that of China, but it is for just this reason that these early Japanese paintings and decorative objects in the Shōsō-in are of such great interest, for they give a reliable picture of the type of painting prevalent at Ch'ang-an during the seventh and eighth centuries.

11

The Heian and Kamakura

Periods

ALTHOUGH few examples have been preserved, there is no doubt that the art of the landscape continued to develop rapidly during the early Heian, or Jōgan, period in the ninth century. Numerous literary references attest to this, and names of famous artists, such as Kudara no Kawanari and Kose no Kanaoka, are frequently mentioned. The former is said to have painted landscapes on the walls of the Seiryō-den of the Imperial Palace in Kyoto, and the latter seems to have been primarily a landscape painter. Their work has not survived, but presumably it reflected the style of the late T'ang dynasty, a period during which important advances were made in the art of the landscape.

A turbulent civil war in China interrupted the relations between the Japanese and the T'ang court, and the influence of Chinese art gradually declined. A more native Japanese style emerged, and we are told that pure landscapes with wholly Japanese scenes were painted. In 838 the last official Japanese embassy was sent to the T'ang court, and during the next centuries there were only sporadic and individual contacts, chiefly by monks and merchants. The result of this cultural isolation was the growth in the arts of a strong national tradition during the Heian, or Fujiwara, period (894—1185), a development which finds its noblest expression in a school of painting known as Yamato-e, or "Japanese painting," which is regarded as the very essence of the Japanese style. Later schools, such as the Tosa and the Sumiyoshi, are derived from it, and to this very day it continues to flourish among the Japanese-style painters. The salient characteristic of the Yamato-e is a strong emphasis upon narrative, and most of the paintings of this type are *e-makimono,* or hand scrolls, relating the history of some famous person or of some celebrated temple. Besides the narrative, there is also a pronounced emphasis upon the decorative quality of the scene portrayed, especially in the scrolls of the Heian period, such as the celebrated *Genji Monogatari,* or "Tale of Genji," scroll. Landscapes, if compared to contemporary Chinese ones, are of minor importance, appearing largely as a setting for the people, although probably the pure landscape also existed.[92]

There are today no tenth-century originals, but the wall paintings at the Byōdō-in may give some idea of how the landscapes of the eleventh century looked. The building itself was completed in 1053, and it is believed that the paintings, which today are badly damaged, were executed at the same time.[93] Although the scenes are primarily Buddhist, the landscape setting is a very important part of the compositions. The dominant color scheme is a rich, soft green, and the hills, which are gracefully rounded, in keeping with the countryside around Kyoto, stand in striking contrast to the towering landscapes which Chinese painters were creating. There is a gentle, decorative beauty in these works, something very charming and typically Japanese. Judging from the literary accounts, as well as from the landscapes on the screen shown in the twelfth-century *Genji Monogatari* scroll,[94] this type of colorful landscape must have been quite common at the time.

The most outstanding example of a Heian period landscape painting is the six-fold screen at the Kyōōgokoku-ji *(Plate 75),* a temple in Kyoto popularly known as Tō-ji. According to temple tradition, the screen was brought back from China during the ninth century by Kōbō Daishi as a gift of the T'ang Emperor Hsien-tsung, and another tradition attributes the work to the twelfth-century priest Chinkai.[95] It is generally believed that the screen which we have today is a twelfth- or, as some scholars think, eleventh-century version of the ninth-century screen, the copy probably having been made after the original had been damaged. In any case, the work shows certain T'ang characteristics, particularly in the costumes of the figures, but it is very Japanese in its use of color and in the treatment of the landscape, especially in the gently-curving hills and the green trees with delicate foliage. Its subject is that of a young nobleman visiting a hermit, but while the figures and the horse and even the inside of the hut are all painted in careful detail, the greater part of the screen is devoted to the landscape which, viewed from a high point, stretches back in a panorama of hills, trees, a large body of water, and a band of sky.

This type of landscape screen, called *senzui byōbu*, is used by the esoteric Shingon sects in connection with the *kanjō*, a religious ceremony during which the priest is given his wand. The ceremony is of Indian origin, and we are told:

On the occasion of the formal nomination or ascension of an heir to the throne, water taken from the four great seas was poured over the head of the heir as a symbol of blessing. A map of the whole kingdom was hung at the hall to show that the heir is the ruler over all these regions. This ceremony was adopted by the Buddhist priests of the esoteric sects in an initiation in which the secrets of the sect were disclosed to a person. The landscape screen is considered to be a modification of the map used for the Abhiseka in ancient India.[96]

Another work painted in a quite similar style is the "Iron Pagoda" in the Fujita collection in Osaka,[97] which is probably from the eleventh century. Although it is a Buddhist painting, the landscape is very prominent and shows the same style with the same color scheme—a soft green in the hills and a darker shade for the trees. The space is so shallow that the hills appear to be piled on top of each other, and there is little emphasis on the atmosphere. This and the strong decorative quality would suggest a date sometime in the eleventh rather than the twelfth century, when there was more emphasis upon space.

Of all the works of the Heian period and the subsequent Kamakura period, the most typical are the narrative scrolls, or *e-makimono*. One of the oldest and finest of these is the *Shigisan Engi*, or "History of Mt. Shigi," scroll which comes from the very end of the Fujiwara period and is owned by the

Chōgosonshi-ji in Nara *(Plate 76)*. It illustrates very clearly the most out-standing trait of the Yamato-e, for the prime emphasis is upon the narrative rather than the grandeur of the landscape, which to the Chinese artist of the twelfth century would have seemed all-important. The hills, the trees, the deer, and the road are all beautifully painted, yet the figures, though they occupy only a small part of the scene, are the real center of interest. Everything about them attracts the eye—their gait, their gestures, their appearance of lively conversation, as well as the manner in which they are painted; one figure is almost without color, and the other exhibits a contrasting of dark and light tones, as in the hair against the hat and in the flowers on the sleeve of the extended arm. The decorative element which had been so pronounced during the Fujiwara period is here not stressed as much, suggesting that this work already anticipates a style which is usually associated with the Kamakura period.

It must be pointed out that even this very Japanese type of painting shows a certain dependence upon China, since the idea of the narrative scroll probably goes back to Chinese prototypes of the T'ang period. Even among works of the same age there is a certain similarity, and one can find parallels between this detail of the *Shigisan Engi* scroll and the autumn landscape from the Liao tomb in eastern Mongolia, which was discussed in the chapter on Northern Sung painting. Not only is the subject matter of the mountains and deer similar, but also the style itself, with its emphasis upon the freely-rendered lines of the undulating hills. However, the two figures engaged in animated discussion while they walk up the road are typically Japanese, both in the emphasis upon genre and in the rather humorous approach to the subject.

The Yamato-e style reached its highest development during the Kama-kura period (1185—1333), and a large number of thirteenth-century scrolls have been preserved. However, in most of them the figures are so dominant that the landscapes are little more than a setting. It is interesting to note that Japanese painting emphasizes landscape most when it is most under the influence of Chinese art, while the more purely Japanese schools, like the Yamato-e, the Sōtatsu School, or the Ukiyo-e tend to stress the decorative and narrative elements. It was only at the end of the Kamakura period

90

that the landscape, again influenced by the Chinese, reappeared in its pure form. Scrolls such as the *Ippen Shōnin Eden* by Hōgen En-i, which is dated 1299 and is in the Kangikō-ji in Kyoto,[98] and the *Saigyō Monogatari* scroll in the Ohara collection in Okayama[99] show, in their greater emphasis upon atmosphere and space, a new dependence on Chinese models. There is no doubt that by the end of the Kamakura period Sung painting had begun to reach Japan and that it was exerting an influence which was to become dominant during the fourteenth and fifteenth centuries.

The purest Kamakura landscapes are not found on narrative scrolls but on screens and *kakemono,* or hanging scrolls. Of these probably the most outstanding is the *senzui byōbu* of Jingo-ji in Kyoto, which represents a nobleman who has come to visit a lady living in a villa among the mountains *(Plate 77).* The human activity is again subordinate, even more so than it was in the Tō-ji screen, for while in the earlier work the hermit and the young nobleman with his retainers were placed in a prominent position in the center foreground, in the later work the figures are so tiny and so scattered that it is difficult to tell which among the various groups is the most important. The entire scene consists of six panels, three of which have been rearranged here in what must be the proper order. Their sequence today is obviously wrong, and one can only assume that they were incorrectly reassembled after the work had been repaired.[100] Since the landscape is an autumn scene, it is believed that this *byōbu* was originally one of four screens representing the four seasons. The style is that of the Yamato-e School of the thirteenth century, and the same colorful treatment of the mountains may be found in the scroll paintings of the period as well as the multitude of details. Here, for example, one can see the baskets of the tiny figures in the upper right, and in the lower right the rein on the horse's neck, the palings in the fence behind, and the floor boards of the narrow verandah which runs around the house, yet at the same time the screen has a sense of space and grandeur which is not found in the narrative scrolls. In this way it goes back to works like the Tō-ji screen, although there is a greater feeling of depth in the Kamakura painting. The scene is again viewed from above, but here the point of view shifts so that different parts of the landscape are seen from different levels.

Of the *kakemono* of this period the most remarkable is the one of the Nachi Waterfall which is now in the Nezu collection in Tokyo *(Plate 78)*. Traditionally attributed to Kose no Kanaoka, it is certainly not that early but rather a work of the thirteenth century. Although it appears to be a pure landscape, it is in actuality a religious painting which represents one of the Kumano shrines and is therefore called a Kumano *mandara*. No black and white reproduction can give any adequate idea of this wonderful painting: while the boldness of the design comes through, the effect of the beautiful colors—deep brown in the rocks, various greens in the foliage, dark brown shading to red in the sun—is lost. If one compares this work to contemporary Sung paintings, one sees at once the difference between the typically Chinese and the typically Japanese style. A Sung artist would have had a sage contemplating the mystery of the falling water as a symbol both of the eternal flux and the ultimate essence, but the Japanese painter is more interested in the formal decorative aspects, such as the vertical movement of the white water against the dark rocks and the green of the trees against the glowing sun. In Chinese painting man always has a place, however tiny, in the vast and mysterious cosmos, while in this work there is no sign of man at all—nothing but the cascade, which is meant to represent Hiryū-gongen, the god of the Nachi Waterfall. There is also a very great difference in the use of space: while the Chinese artist tried to create an endlessly receding depth in order to suggest the vastness of the universe, the Japanese painter used a shallow space which brings out the more decorative character of the painting. Perhaps the most important of all is the different treatment of line and color: while the Sung artist, working primarily with line, used a monochrome, the Japanese artist emphasized areas of bright color.

It has already been said that this painting is called a *mandara,* and since it is of the type usually associated with the Kasuga Shrine in Nara, these paintings are known as Kasuga *mandara*'s. They are expressions of a religious sect, the Suijaku, which represents the merging of Shinto and Buddhist thought so popular during the period. The most common Kasuga *mandara*'s show the shrine with the Mikasa hills in the background.[101] The treatment of the landscape is usually highly stylized, with little feeling of depth or atmosphere, and there are bright colors—reds, gold, and silver—for the

92

painter is more interested in the decorative effect and in the rendering of the sacred sanctuaries than in the landscape, since these *kakemono* were regarded as cult images and, through them, the deities were worshipped. In fact, in many the deities themselves are shown in human form.

During the opening years of the fourteenth century, at the close of the Kamakura period, Zen priests began to introduce monochrome landscape painting from Sung China. However, as far as is known, it did not have any immediate effect upon the native schools, and it was only in the following period that this type of painting became the dominant artistic influence in Japan.

12

The Muromachi Period

UNDER the impact of Zen Buddhism, which during the Muromachi, or Ashikaga, period (1333—1573) enjoyed a tremendous popularity in Japan, the art of the landscape flourished as never before. Not only did Zen monks bring back Sung and Yüan landscape scrolls from the Chinese mainland, but also Japanese painters such as Sesshū visited China to study her art. Like the Southern Sung period, the Muromachi was an age of political unrest, yet in the very midst of the decline there was a wonderful flowering of the arts. Monuments such as the Golden Pavilion, or Kinkaku-ji, built by the Ashikaga Shogun Yoshimitsu, are a testament to the brilliance of the age, and the beautiful gardens, the cult of the tea ceremony, and above all, the wonderful monochrome ink paintings are all evidence of the highly developed taste. The eighth Ashikaga Shogun, Yoshimasa, was an illustrious patron of the arts, and the catalogue of his magnificent collection, the *Kintaikan Sayūchōki,* which was compiled by Sōami and contains a description of the shogun's paintings and ceramics, is still studied today.

The cultural dependence upon China was so great during this period that Chinese pictures, imported in large numbers, were "frequently used as gifts, given and received for the promotion of social intercourse. Especially, it was customary that the tribute offered to the Shogun must always include pictures, and these pictures were almost always those imported from China, just as the implements used on such occasions were all Chinese. Again, the gifts from the Shogun, those interchanged by warriors, Zen priests and others on important occasions, chiefly consisted of Chinese pictures."[102]

The first decades of the period were torn by bloody strife, but after the settlement of the civil war in 1392 Kyoto once again became a center of artistic activity, with painting flourishing in the Zen monasteries. The earliest of these *suiboku,* or "water and ink," landscapists were Minchō, also known as Chō Denso (1352—1431), and Josetsu, who was active during the early part of the fifteenth century. It is not by chance that both artists were Zen priests, for there was a very close relation between this sect and the new type of painting. A landscape of Minchō entitled "Hermitage by the Mountain Brook" and dated 1413 is preserved in the Konchi-in in Kyoto,[103] while the only certain work of Josetsu is a painting from around 1417 which is called "Catching a Catfish with a Gourd" and is owned by the Taizō-in, also in Kyoto.[104] These two early fifteenth-century scrolls are interesting, not so much as works of art (for the style had not yet been fully developed), but as evidence of the intimate relation between these artists and those of the Southern Sung period. Unlike the landscapes of the Yamato-e masters, theirs were often not Japanese scenes at all but rather imaginary Chinese landscapes. The most famous subject was the eight views of the Hsiao and Hsiang Rivers, or *Sho-sho-hakkei* in Japanese, the same one which had been so popular with the Southern Sung painters, while another Chinese-inspired scene was the imaginary view of *P'en Lai Shan,* the Island of Everlasting Youth, or *Horai-san,* as the Japanese called it. Such was the impact of Chinese culture and Chinese ideals that not only the style of Japanese painting but also its subject matter was completely transformed by the foreign influence.

Josetsu's importance in the history of Japanese landscape painting depends less upon his own works (of which hardly any have survived) than upon his position as a teacher. We are told that he ran a regular school for *suiboku* painters at the Zen monastery in which he was residing, the Shōkoku-ji in Kyoto, and it was from centers such as this that the new type of painting spread until it became the dominant style of the period. How closely Josetsu's name was linked with this development can best be seen by the fact that the inscription on his "Catching a Catfish with a Gourd" states that it was

96

painted in "the new style" by the order of the Ashikaga Shogun Yoshimochi and that he wished to have it always kept near his seat.

Shūbun, Josetsu's most distinguished pupil, was also a Zen priest at the Shōkoku-ji monastery, and he was apparently able, as were the other painter-priests of the period, to combine his profession as an artist with his priestly calling. The exact dates of his life are not known, but it is believed that his main activity falls into the first half of the fifteenth century, and it is he who is usually regarded as the first great landscape painter of the period. A large number of works have been attributed to him with more or less justice, but while few if any can be assigned to him with certainty, it is clear that his style closely followed Southern Sung models. He is said to have spent a year in Korea around 1423, and after his return he became the leading exponent of *suiboku* painting in Japan, as well as the first artist working in the new Chinese manner, and was made chief government artist for the Ashikaga Shogunate.

Of the many paintings attributed to him, the most convincing are the *kakemono* entitled "Reading in a Hermitage in a Bamboo Grove" in the collection of the National Museum in Tokyo[105] and the mountain landscape owned by Mr. Fujiwara of Tokyo *(Plate 79)*. They are dated 1447 and 1445 respectively and show the artist's style at its best. The earlier one is a typical Southern Sung work done in the style of Hsia Kuei and Ma Yüan or, to use their Japanese names, Kakei and Bayen. Not only is the theme familiar, with the scholar in his little hut, the crooked pines, the rocks, the water, the boats, the mist, and the mountains, but also the spirit of the painting is very much in keeping with the ideals of Kuo Hsi. Apparently the impact of the new art was so overwhelming that in the work of the first generation of *suiboku* painters there is little to indicate that they are Japanese. Shūbun's handling of ink, or *sumi,* with his skillful use of tonal values to suggest space and atmospheric effects and his inspired brushwork in the pines, is worthy of the best of the Southern Sung tradition. Perhaps depth is not emphasized as much as it would have been in its Chinese prototype, but even this difference is not very pronounced. Shūbun's works represent a kind of revival in Japan of the thirteenth-century Chinese style of painting long after it had ceased to be popular in China itself, and it is not surprising that the finest

97

Southern Sung paintings are today in Japan, where they were brought by the avid and discriminating collectors of the Ashikaga period.

It was another generation before this foreign style was absorbed, and although its Chinese derivation was still evident, it was transformed into something decidedly Japanese. The credit for this belongs to Sesshū, the greatest painter of his period and, like many another well-known artist, a pupil of Shūbun at Shōkoku-ji, which at this time was the art center of Kyoto. Like his master, Sesshū too was a Zen monk, but his calling in no way interfered with his devoting himself to his art. Born in 1420, he was at least a generation younger than Shūbun, and he not only absorbed what the Zen masters and *suiboku* painters of Kyoto had to offer, but in 1468 he even succeeded in making the long and arduous trip to China, where he visited, among other places, the Southern Sung capital of Hang-chou and the court at Peking. Apparently he was very disappointed in the contemporary art of China, and he felt that only nature and the masters of the Sung and Yüan periods could teach him anything. It seems unlikely that he saw the works of such outstanding Ming painters as Tai Chin and Shên Chou, for otherwise his harsh judgement would be very surprising. However, it may be that the Japanese whose eye had been trained by studying Sung paintings had as little appreciation of Ming work as the Ming artists themselves had for some of the great Sung masters.

Apparently the Chinese greatly admired Sesshū's genius, for we are told that he was given the first place next to the abbot when he visited the famous T'ien-t'ung Shan temple, one of the great centers of Zen learning, an honor of which he was very proud and later often mentioned in the inscriptions on his paintings. It is also reported by his travelling companion, Ryōshin, that he was commissioned to do a wall painting for the court in Peking. Relating this event eight years after it happened, Ryōshin says:

The minister Yō (Yao K'uei) ordered the venerable Sesshū to paint on the central room of the Ministry of Rites, Peking. He said, "Nowadays, although tribute comes to China from about thirty distant barbarian countries which use strange languages, I have seen no paintings like Sesshū's. Furthermore, as this place is headquarters directing the examinations, there are no notable men in China who will not come to this hall. And when they do, they will call the candidates together and will point to the wall and say, 'This is excellent painting of the honorable Japanese priest, Yō

98

Sesshū.' Even outside-barbarians possess such rare skill. In order to reach this level, why do you not study more diligently at your task." He was thus praised in great China.[106]

Even if this account is somewhat exaggerated, it seems clear that Sesshū did receive recognition in China, and after his return his prestige in his own country was enormous. In fact, his fame was so great that local rulers vied with one another to get him to work for them, and ever since his own period he has been considered one of Japan's greatest artists. There are, no doubt, those who prefer artists who are more distinctly Japanese, but even they cannot deny the strength of Sesshū's brushwork or the power of his genius.

Among the many paintings which today are attributed to Sesshū, the most famous is the long *makimono* in the Mōri collection in Tokyo, a fifty-foot scroll starting with a spring scene and ending with a winter one *(Plate 80)*. Both the subject and the style suggest the influence of Hsia Kuei, but the work itself is highly individual. Painted in 1486, when the artist was sixty-seven years old, it is one of the best examples of his mature style. The brilliance of the brushwork is very striking, the strokes now charged with energy as in the rocks and pines and now muted as in the faintly-indicated trees around the pagoda. His skillful use of ink tones in the rocks in the foreground recalls the style of Li T'ang, whose work he greatly admired, while the influence of Ma Yüan, another of his idols, is evident in the over-hanging branches of the pine, and that of Hsia Kuei, his favorite painter, in the hazy contours of the mountains. Yet the scroll is not completely derivative, for there are certain characteristics which are not found in the work of the Southern Sung painters. The most outstanding of these are the greater emphasis on broad, heavy black outlines, the stronger contrast between ink values, and the more angular line. There is less feeling of depth, and in the treatment of the space itself little of that sense of space as something mysterious. The main emphasis in the scroll is usually on the foreground, where buildings and people are shown in far greater detail than would be customary in Sung painting. Then again, the narrative element which is found in some sections of the scroll may be considered typically Japanese, since it was one of the outstanding characteristics of Yamato-e painting. Although Sesshū was quite consciously in the Chinese tradition, he nevertheless transformed it into a style which has both personal and Japanese characteristics.

While the Mōri work illustrates the so-called *shin* manner following Hsia Kuei and the other masters of the Northern School, the *kakemono* in the National Museum in Tokyo *(Plate 81)* shows the "splashed-ink," or *hatsuboku,* style of the Southern School (called *Nanga* by the Japanese) and especially of Ying Yü-chien (known as Gyokukan in Japan). Painted in 1495, when Sesshū was seventy-six years old, it is a late work of the artist and shows that Sesshū, like many of the masters of other ages, far from declining as he grew old, developed an even more expressive style. A lengthy inscription in the upper part of the scroll, which is not included in the reproduction, says that it was given by the aged Sesshū to his pupil Shūen upon the latter's return to Kamakura.[107]

Although the theme is familiar, the subject has been completely transformed by the style, in which the ink is splashed onto the paper with a very wet brush. It is a free yet inspired manner and so abstract that everything is indicated with the greatest economy. The inn with the wine flag in the right foreground is sketched in with half a dozen strokes, while a few quick lines indicate the two figures in the tiny boat. The weight of the composition falls in the lower half of the painting, where splashy black and grey strokes suggest trees on a cliff, while in the upper part a few pale, narrow peaks hang disembodied. There are strong contrasts between the black ink and the white paper and between the different kinds of strokes, some thin and sharp and others like blots with blurred edges. It is a work which has inspired a host of imitators, and it has long been considered the finest example of Japanese *haboku,* or "broken-ink," painting.

A younger contemporary of Sesshū's was Sōami, the court favorite; he is now believed to have been born in 1472 and to have died in 1526. The son and pupil of Geiami, himself a distinguished painter, and the grandson of the equally distinguished Nōami, he is the third of the San-ami, or the "Three Ami." He spent his entire artistic life at the court of the Ashikaga Shogun Yoshimasa (1449—1490), where he served not only as painter but also as tea master, calligrapher, garden designer, and as we have seen above, art expert. Of the paintings which have survived, the most famous is a set of twenty landscapes owned by the Daisen-in of the Daitoku-ji in Kyoto *(Plate 82)*. The style of those works recalls the manner of Mu-ch'i, or Mokkei, as he was known in Japan, rather than that of Hsia Kuei, a taste in which Sōami was the pioneer. The soft, rounded forms of the hills, the delicate ink tones, the emphasis upon space and atmosphere are certainly very different from the stronger and more expressive style of Sesshū. However, if one compares his work with that of his Chinese model, one notices a stronger contrast of ink tones as well as a greater amount of narrative detail, especially in the multiplication of houses and boats. In spite of these differences, the similarity to Southern Sung painting is very marked, indicating the still close relationship between Chinese and Japanese monochrome ink painting.

Among the men of Sōami's generation, by far the most famous was Kano Motonobu (1476—1559). As the founder of the Kano School he was to exert a profound influence upon Japanese painting of the following centuries. He too was a Zen monk as well as a devoted student of Chinese painting, but his work, while still influenced by Hsia Kuei and Ma Yüan and the other great thirteenth-century painters, also reveals a strong influence of contemporary Ming painting. In fact, the Ming emperor himself, after seeing some of Motonobu's work, praised it in the following letter:

I have seen your productions, which were sent to this country by yourself. They display such masterly skill as to suffice to make them rival even the pictures by Ch'ao Ch'ang or those of Ma Yüan. If you will come to my country, I shall esteem it a privilege to be permitted to become your pupil.[108]

In spite of these influences, Motonobu was at the same time a typically Japanese artist. He had been brought up in the Yamato-e tradition and he had married the daughter of Tosa Mitsunobu, thus becoming the heir of the Tosa School in regard to certain artistic privileges and functions at the court of the shogun, and due to this the Kano School became the official one, a status it enjoyed during the entire Tokugawa period. The new elements he introduced are at once apparent in the scroll entitled "Priest Ling-yün Viewing Peach Blossoms," a typical Kano School work attributed to Motonobu which is now in the National Museum in Tokyo but was originally in the Founder's Hall at Daisen-in *(Plate 83)*. The subject is Chinese, showing a famous Chinese Zen priest who achieved enlightenment while looking at

101

the peach blossoms, but the treatment is typically Japanese in the Kano tradition. The two qualities which are most pronounced are the strong decorative character and the marked realism of detail. Distance and atmosphere, which had been all important in Sung painting, are here hardly noticeable, for the space is shallow, and everything—twigs, blades of glass, leaves—is very sharply defined. This gives it a hard, rather tight quality which is typical of much of the work of the Kano School. The waterfall, the tree, and the rocks are all treated in a stylized manner which shows little feeling for the growth of natural things. It is an explicit statement very different from the elusive suggestions of the great Southern Sung masters, yet it is this very quality which later Kano painters developed into a kind of academic formula.

Besides this kind of painting, Motonobu also worked in a more Chinese style, an example of which is his famous set of paintings in the Reiun-in of the Myōshin-ji in Kyoto, a famous Zen temple in which Motonobu once lived for a time.[109] In these he worked in the manner of Hsia Kuei, Ma Yüan, Mu Ch'i, and Ying Yü-chien, although he modified their styles in the light of Japanese taste. This set is the most frequently reproduced of all his works, but it is less characteristic of the pure Kano style than the painting in the National Museum discussed here. Other works of his are executed in a typical Tosa manner with bright colors and Japanese subjects, but even these as well as his most Chinese paintings show something of the new spirit of the Kano School, which was to dominate the official art of the Edo period.

The last great painter of the Muromachi period was Sesson, who lived from 1504 to 1589. Although he was born too late to have actually studied under Sesshū, he became one of the most gifted of his many imitators. Like the other great artists of the time, he was a Zen priest who worked in the *suiboku* style associated with this sect. His masterpiece, a very small painting on paper owned by Mr. Nomura of Kyoto, is a stormy lake scene, painted with a boldness and expressive power seldom equalled even by Sesshū himself *(Plate 84)*. The composition is very striking, with the weight of the area in the left foreground, a bank broken by the sharp vertical of a tree and balanced by the boat which is set deep in the right half of the picture. Everything contributes to the feeling of the storm—the sail straining at its ropes, the huddled figures, the branches bent by the wind—yet it is all done with great simplicity. Around the boat a series of light, sketchy lines indicate the swell of the waves, and the merging of water and sky by the use of soft, subtly-varied tones is enough to suggest the storm itself. Unfortunately, the other works of Sesson do not live up to this masterpiece, but even so he is undoubtedly the last great painter of his period.

The heights achieved by the landscape during the two centuries of the Muromachi age were never equalled in any of the following periods. Men like Shūbun, Sesshū, Motonobu, and Sesson are among the greatest painters Japan has ever produced, and there are others of real distinction who could not be included in this brief discussion. It is interesting that the emergence of the landscape as the most important genre of painting goes hand in hand with a marked Chinese influence and that this is not only true during the Muromachi period but also during the Nara period, when the landscape was of major importance, and again during the Edo period, when, under Chinese influence, the Nanga School emerged. On the other hand, the schools which show the most distinctly Japanese traits such as Yamato-e, the Sōtatsu-Kōrin School, and Ukiyo-e emphasize landscape less and figure-painting more. Hence it would seem as if the pure landscape was not a native Japanese expression.

13

The Momoyama Period

THE strong Chinese influence so characteristic of Muromachi landscape painting did not continue in the subsequent Momoyama period (1574–1614), which developed a Japanese style with the emphasis on the decorative quality of the painting. It is indicative that the great artists were no longer Zen monks creating in the quiet of some temple compound, but professional artists who worked for the great military leaders of the day, men such as Nobunaga and Hideyoshi. In fact, the period begins with the erection of Nobunaga's magnificent seven-story castle at Azuchi on the southern shore of Lake Biwa, and it is named after the Momoyama, or "Peach Hill," near Kyoto, where Hideyoshi had his castle built in 1594. Both were decorated with a wealth of splendid paintings, some of which were in monochrome, but most of which were painted in brilliant colors against rich gold-leaf backgrounds. This kind of painting, which was known as *shōhekiga* in contrast to the *kakemono* and *makimono* so prevalent during the Ashikaga period, was used to cover standing screens, or *byōbu; fusuma,* the sliding partitions between rooms; *shōji,* the sliding outer partitions; and the inside walls of the building.

The most celebrated of the great Momoyama painters was Kano Eitoku (1543–1590), the grandson of Kano Motonobu, and it was he who was commissioned to do the decorations in most of the castles. Although trained by his grandfather in the monochrome style of the Ashikaga period, he developed a manner all his own which, with its ornate splendor, gave perfect expression to the wealth and power of the age. In fact, he was the leading artist of the period, and he was not only court painter to Nobunaga but also to Hideyoshi. Unfortunately an early death cut short his career, but even this brief time was enough for him to make an enduring impression on Momoyama art.

There are few works today which can be attributed to him with any certainty. Among the monochrome panels of his early period the most authentic are the series of *fusuma* in the Jukō-in in Kyoto done in the style of Motonobu, though with a greater decorative emphasis.[110] The folding screen with *hinoki* (cypress trees) in the National Museum in Tokyo,[111] which is believed to have originally come from the Azuchi castle, is an example of his mature work showing a characteristically Momoyama style; an even better example is the pair of six-fold screens with hawks and pines in the collection of the University of Arts in Tokyo *(Plate 85)*. Neither of these is a landscape in the pure sense, but it is typical of Momoyama taste that the landscape declined in importance. In this way, the painting resembles that of the Fujiwara period, in which decorative qualities were also emphasized, and Japanese critics have pointed out that Momoyama painting does indeed derive from Yamato-e. However, despite the similarity of brilliant colors and decorative effects, there is a very great difference in that Fujiwara painting is restrained and delicate when compared with the more flamboyant Momo-yama style. It must be said that this ornateness never degenerates into mere vulgarity, for Hideyoshi, in spite of his fondness for display, was also interested in the tea ceremony and in the traditional arts of Japan. These two tendencies, the one towards the splendidly decorative and the other towards simplicity and restraint, exist side by side both in the character of the Japanese and in their artistic tradition. It is thus not as surprising as it would seem at first that the Kano School embraced both tendencies without any sense that they were contradictory. In fact, the work of Eitoku himself reveals the two qualities, for he continued painting in the *suiboku* manner after he had begun to work in the more typical Momoyama style.

The scene with the hawks and pines is a perfect expression of the ornate tendency. Only a good color plate could reproduce the splendor of the

106

original, with the deep greens and blues set off against the gold of the clouds and the white snow, and the sharp black outlines enclosing the areas of brilliant color. There is neither depth nor atmosphere—instead, the shallow space of Japanese tradition has been flattened until it is nearly two dimensional. The emphasis is entirely on the foreground, with the fierce, handsome hawk and the great tree dominating the rocks and the water and especially the distant mountains, a striking contrast to the Chinese works where the mountains tower over the whole painting. Another aspect which is lost in reproduction is the size of the work, for these screens, designed to decorate vast palaces rather than the quiet *tokonoma* of a teahouse, were always tremendous in scale, with the figures nearly life-size.

Perhaps the most typical work of the period is the famous pair of folding screens showing the bridge at Uji, or *Uji-bashi,* as it is called in Japanese *(Plate 86)*. This work was so popular that no less than ten versions of it are extant today, suggesting that many more must have existed at the time. Since one of these versions has the signature of Hasegawa Tōhaku, some scholars have ascribed the original painting to him, but in view of his other work this seems unlikely. In any case, it is one of the most magnificent of the Momoyama paintings, showing all the outstanding characteristics of the period. The subject, a simple one of willows and a bridge crossing the Uji River, has been treated so that the emphasis is entirely upon the formal design. All the components of the picture have been reduced to flat, two-dimensional areas which are arranged in a pattern that no longer has very much resemblance to nature. The bridge seems to rise up into the air, and the clouds, which have small, evenly scalloped edges, look as if they were lying on the water. The waves themselves are reduced to a stylized, scale-like pattern, and the black of the trees against the gold turns the willows into flat silhouettes.

It is probably the emphasis upon design which makes this painting so appealing to modern critics. In any case, its style is certainly typically Japanese, bearing no resemblance either to the Sung landscapes or to the work being produced in contemporary Ming China. It goes back instead to the decorative scrolls of the Yamato-e School, such as the *Genji Monogatari* and *Itsukushima* scrolls, and it also recalls the designs on the lacquer boxes of the Heian and Kamakura periods. In the Momoyama screen, however, the decorative pattern has a new boldness and power. The black curves of the trees, the net-like design of the twigs and delicate leaves, and the diagonal sweep of the bridge are all combined in a compelling pattern. It has none of the poetry or the depth of Sung painting, but for sheer beauty of color and design there are few works anywhere to equal it.

A painter who studied under Eitoku but who was later influenced by Sung and Yüan painters, especially Liang K'ai, was Yūshō (1533—1615). Like the other artists of the period, he did not paint very many landscapes, but at least one of his major works, the pair of screens with fishing nets hung up to dry (now in the National Museum in Tokyo), may be considered a landscape if the term is used in its broadest sense *(Plate 87)*. The work combines very effectively the decorative emphasis of Momoyama painting with the more restrained and poetic spirit of the Sung artists, yet even in this work, the pattern is the strongest element. It is the repeated triangles of the nets which dominate the picture, and the water and the sky, far from suggesting the mystery of space, help to create the formal pattern. The dark bands in the upper right balance the nets in the left foreground, and the relatively undifferentiated stretch of water is broken up by the intricate criss-cross of the reeds at the right. Here again, this painting may lack the profundity of the Sung works which Yūshō admired, but in spite of this it has a distinct beauty of its own.

There were those among the painters who, instead of following the Kano School, turned back to Sesshū for their inspiration. Among these, the most outstanding was Hasegawa Tōhaku (1539—1610), the founder of the Hasegawa School. His relations to Sesshū consisted mainly of his interest in the classical *suiboku* painting, and in spite of the fact that he called himself the Fifth Sesshū, his own style was really closer to that of Mu-ch'i, or Mokkei in Japanese. Among his paintings the most beautiful is undoubtedly the pair of screens with pines which is now in the National Museum in Tokyo, yet even here, where he is using the technique of the Zen artists (and Tōhaku himself was a priest), the basic conception is characteristic of the Momoyama period *(Plate 88)*. Groups of trees, all pines, are isolated against a misty background, and within each group there is a variation of tone from black to grey. The setting has been almost entirely eliminated,

108

and the trees, which are painted on a very large scale, make subtly varied patterns against the white ground. The delicate monochrome style is certainly more restrained than that of the hawk and pine or the Uji Bridge screens, yet basically it shows the same love of the dramatically decorative which characterizes the other screens. It is at once bold and sensitive and, in this way, combines the best of both Chinese and Japanese traditions.

Among the artists who followed Sesshū more closely, the most outstanding was Unkoku Tōgan (1547—1618), the founder of the Unkoku School. He called himself the Sesshū of the Third Generation and set up his quarters in his predecessor's temple-studio, but his work, which has little to recommend it, illustrates the danger of copying another painter's style. He borrowed without adding anything of his own, and as a result his landscapes are merely a weak reflection of his master's.

Although the Momoyama period was the shortest in the history of Japanese art, it is not only one of the most creative, but also one of the most typically Japanese. Its strength lies in the boldness of its color and design, yet in this very strength lies its weakness, for in the last analysis, these paintings, so splendid as decoration, lack the spiritual depth of really great art.

14

The Edo Period

THE brief Momoyama period came to an end in 1616 when Ieyasu Tokugawa, the third of the great military rulers of the age, consolidated his power
and established the Tokugawa shogunate, which was to last for two hundred
and fifty years. Since the Tokugawa shoguns moved their seat of government
to Tokyo, at that time called Edo, this period is usually referred to as the
Edo period, although it may also be called the Tokugawa period. It was an
era of national isolation during which the Tokugawa shoguns not only cut
Japan off from almost every foreign contact, but also refused to permit their
subjects ever to leave the country. These strict regulations, however, had
surprisingly little effect upon art, for it shows the influence of both Chinese
and European styles.

The official art school of the period, the one which enjoyed the patronage
of the shoguns, was the Kano School. It was still run by the descendents of
Kano Masanobu and Kano Motonobu, the original founders, and members
of the family continued the school into modern times. It is characteristic of
the Japanese that schools should be connected with families rather than
particular places or styles, and this was considered so important that if a
family had no son, a favorite pupil would be adopted in order to continue the
name. Students would gather around a famous master, who would then
found his own school, but this does not necessarily mean that all the artists

of the group would work in the same manner. As we have already seen, Kano Eitoku developed a style quite independent from that of his grandfather, Motonobu, and his grandsons, in turn, worked in a style very different from his. Then again, it was not uncommon for a painter to vary his style according to the subject matter, so that an artist of the Kano School might use the Kano style for traditional Chinese subjects, such as the seven sages of the bamboo grove, and then change to the style of the Tosa School when painting such characteristically Japanese subjects as the *Genji Monogatari*. The result is an overlapping which is further complicated by some artists studying with a variety of masters and using different styles at different stages of their development.

The most outstanding of the Kano painters of the Edo period was Kano Naonobu (1607—1650), grandson of Kano Eitoku and brother of Kano Tanyū (1602—1674). He is particularly noted as a painter of landscapes, the most outstanding of which is a pair of screens in the National Museum in Tokyo representing the eight views of the Hsiao and Hsiang Rivers during the summer and the winter seasons *(Plate 89)*. He uses a style reminiscent of the great Southern Sung painter Ying Yü-chien, though the ink is not splashed as freely, nor is the effect of the whole as abstract. Though there are parts, especially in the mountains, where the ink is applied in loose areas, there are other parts where the brushwork is more precise. The pagoda visible behind the peaks in the background, and the little figures and boats, as well as certain branches, are picked out sharply against lighter washes. Blacks contrast with whites, and much of the paper is left blank to suggest space. There is a certain narrative interest in the activites of the figures, but they are so tiny that they are nearly lost in the vast and mysterious space. The fact that the artist became a priest may well be indicative of his desire to follow the example of his great Zen predecessors.

Of the two brothers the elder, Kano Tanyū, was not only the more famous but also the favorite artist of the shogun, and it was he who was to influence the Kano painters for generations to come. His style varies according to the subject, but generally it shows the influence of Motonobu and the Sesshū School. However, most of his work is rather academic, with a stiffness and angular hardness in the brush stroke which was to become even more pronounced in his many followers. Since Neo-Confusianism was regarded very highly by the Tokugawa shoguns, the subjects for his paintings were often taken from Chinese history and literature. A typical work of his, which is in the National Museum in Tokyo, is the folding screen of a lake scene showing a famous Chinese scholar admiring the lotus plants.[112] In its realism the style resembles contemporary Ming painting, but it is characteristic of the Kano School in its decorative use of bright gold. A work illustrating his use of Japanese subjects is the triptych of Mt. Fuji in the same museum.[113]

In spite of the prestige and success of the Kano School, the most important creative work was not done by Kano painters but by artists belonging to rival schools. The one closest to the native Japanese tradition was the Sōtatsu School, which in some ways followed the ideals of Yamato-e. Little is known about the life of Sōtatsu himself, and even his dates are uncertain, although it is known that his artistic activity falls roughly in the first half of the seventeenth century and it is believed that he died in 1643. There are almost no real landscapes among his works, for the artists of this school usually painted figure compositions or decorative flower pieces. The only pure landscape attributed to him is the screen in the Freer Gallery in Washington showing Matsushima Bay with its rocky islands.[114] The emphasis is almost entirely upon the decorative design, with the animated linear pattern of the tempestuous waves set off against the solid mass of the islands. There is nothing here of that mystical serenity which pervades the great Zen painting, nor is there much illusion of reality, for the artist is so interested in the abstract quality of the lines and shapes and colors that he loses sight of the actual scene itself. The emphasis upon abstract art in our own time has brought about a re-evaluation of Sōtatsu, and today he is much admired.

Sōtatsu's most famous and, at the same time, most typical work is a pair of screens in the Seikadō showing episodes from the *Genji Monogatari*[115] *(Plate 90)*. In these scenes the landscape is almost wholly incidental to the figures, but this is true of nearly all his paintings. The flat, decorative use of areas of bright color and the lack of emphasis upon the brush strokes recalls the manner of the early Yamato-e artists, but Sōtatsu has a simplicity and strength of design which they were lacking. Even in the detail one can see how strong the composition is with the elongated S-curve of the beach

113

swinging from the tree at the lower right to the tree at the upper left. The people themselves are arranged in a narrower S-curve, and variations of the same figure are repeated in the trunks of the pines. Although the foreground is filled with people, it does not seem crowded, because he reduced the people to areas of flat, simple color. The treatment of the pines, where the needles, instead of being indicated by separate strokes, are massed together in dark, solid areas, is reminiscent of Momoyama painting, but this is not surprising, since Sōtatsu's artistic career began in the Momoyama period. Here again, the black and white reproduction results in a tremendous loss, for one of the most important aspects of the painting is the contrast of the colors against the white sand and the gold of the ground.

Unlike the Kano masters, Sōtatsu did not at once gather a school around him, but Ogata Kōrin (1663—1743), another great artist, continued his style a century later. Interestingly enough, Kōrin, in his "Waves at Matsushima" screen, now in the Boston Museum of Fine Arts,[116] took up the same subject which Sōtatsu had painted. The style is quite similar to that of the older artist, but Kōrin adds to the animation of the design by multiplying the waves and rocks so that there is a strong feeling of dynamic movement. The green of the foliage stands out brilliantly against the gold of the sky and the gold and white of the waves, and the swirl of the water with its splashing foam is particularly effective.

As in the case of Sōtatsu, this work is rather isolated, for Kōrin rarely painted landscapes and, when he did, they were usually settings which were treated in a simplified and abstract manner. Typical of this kind of landscape is his famous pair of two-part screens with flowering plum trees in the Tsugaru collection in Tokyo, a work which embodies the Japanese love for the decorative in its purest form *(Plate 91)*. The emphasis is entirely upon the two-dimensional pattern, and there is no attempt to convey any illusion of space or atmosphere. The effect of this, combined with the gorgeous colors, is very similar to a lacquer design, a medium in which Kōrin also excelled. The background is gold, and the water, which seems to stand straight up in the air, was done in silver leaf, now unfortunately darkened. The spiralling ripples of the stream were painted in gold ink, and there are white blossoms at the left and pink blossoms at the right against

114

trunks which are dark brown with green. The whole is very artificial, yet at the same time it reveals a close study of nature, especially in the way the plum trees branch and in the tiny leaves and in the buds and flowers springing directly from the twigs.

The most outstanding school of landscape painters during the eighteenth century was strongly influenced by Chinese art and ideals. The new style, called Nanga, or "Southern Painting," was based on the Southern School of Chinese painting, expecially the great masters of the Sung, Yüan, and early Ch'ing periods. The defeat of the native Ming dynasty by the foreign Manchu rulers had led some Chinese artists to seek refuge in Japan, and through Nagasaki, which served as a center of foreign commerce, Chinese paintings and books on art criticism reached Japan. Interest in things Chinese was further stimulated by the fact that during the Tokugawa period there was an emphasis upon Confucian learning as well as upon the Chinese classics.

The painting which these artists practiced was called *bunjinga,* or "gentlemen's painting," a Japanese version of the *wên jên hua* of the Ming and Ch'ing periods. Here, as in China, the artists were supposed to be dilettantes in the best sense of the word, literati and scholars who painted for their amusement and inspiration rather than to earn a livelihood. How close their relationship was to their Chinese models is illustrated by the fact that the poems and lengthy inscriptions which they often added to their scrolls were usually in Chinese rather than Japanese. To them calligraphy was an art equal to painting, so that poem and picture were considered parts of an inseparable whole. Characteristically enough, this school was particularly popular in Kyoto, the old cultural center, rather than in Edo, where the Kano and the Ukiyo-e Schools flourished.

The most celebrated of the eighteenth-century Nanga painters was Ikeno Taiga, who lived from 1723 to 1776 and whose last work is a series of album leaves, which is in the collection of Mr. Kawabata in Kamakura *(Plate 92).* The paintings are illustrations for a poem by the Chinese Ch'ing poet Li Li-wêng, entitled *Jū Ben Jū Gi* in Japanese, or the "Ten Conveniences and Ten Enjoyments [of Rural Life]," written in reply to a friend who had expressed sympathy for the inconveniences of the country life the poet was leading. The *Jū Ben* was illustrated by Taiga, while the illustrations for the *Jū Gi*

115

were done at the same time by Buson, the second most famous of the Nanga painters. The very fact that the picture is based on a Chinese poem is already indicative of the ideals of the Nanga School, and it is also interesting that Taiga was as well known for his calligraphy as he was for his painting. The style of this work, which is so simple that it is almost abstract, resembles that of some of the early Ch'ing painters, such as Shih-t'ao. Compared to the Sōtatsu School with its emphasis upon areas of decorative color, the painting is subdued and linear. There are pale greens and blues in the fields, bluish greys in the trees, and a soft brown in the house.[117] Individual brush strokes are once again apparent; they are very generalized, summing up rather than describing, with short repeated strokes representing the plants in the tiny plots and heavier, looser strokes indicating the trees. The house, like the ones Ni Tsan had painted, is reduced to a few lines, and at the left, behind the roof, a shadowy area represents trees in the distance obscured by haze. There is a quiet sense of beauty in the painting, for Taiga, like the Ashikaga masters, was interested in the world of nature. However, he does not experience it as something mystical or overwhelming, for he sees it through the eyes of a cultured gentleman-painter who finds a charm in the pleasures of rural life.

The most inspired of all the Nanga painters was Uragami Gyokudō (1745 —1820), an artist somewhat younger than Taiga. His work until recently was rather neglected, but due to its affinity to certain aspects of modern painting, he has been much admired by contemporary critics. A typical example of his style is a mountain landscape in the Yamaguchi collection in Kyoto *(Plate 93),* which resembles the work of Shih-t'ao, especially the album leaf discussed in the chapter on Ch'ing painting. In both there is the same freedom and spontaneity of brushwork as well as the same eccentric but inspired quality. The actual forms of the individual objects are no longer so important as the beauty and expressiveness of the ink tones themselves, as for example the towering range of nearer mountains, painted in masses of black, and the trees in the foreground, with their swift strokes and splashes. There is the same kind of abstraction which many artists today use, and it is this which gives the work a modern appeal. These two men, Gyokudō and Taiga, stand well above the majority of Nanga painters, for, like many

116

of the early Ch'ing artists, most were rather uninspired, treating landscapes in a dull and traditional way.

Probably the most representative painter of eighteenth-century Japan was Maruyama Ōkyo, who was born in 1733 and died in 1795. Originally a Kano-style painter, he later studied Western perspective as well as the realistic manner of the Ming artists and combined these with the decorative spirit of Japanese painting. The result was a kind of decorative realism which was immensely popular in his own time and has continued so up to the present day, and the Maruyama School he founded was one of the most important of the Edo period. Its ideals were opposed to the ideals of the official Kano School, with its emphasis upon tradition, and to those of the Chinese-inspired Nanga School, for to Ōkyo the only master was nature. As he said:

A painting which is not a faithful copy of nature has neither beauty nor is worthy of the name art. What I mean to say is this: be the subject what it may, a landscape, a bird, a bullock, a tree, a stone, or an insect, it should be treated in a way so life-like that it is instinct with life and motion. Now this is beyond the possiblity of any other art save that of the West. Judged from this point of view, Japanese and Chinese paintings look very puerile, hardly deserving the name of art.[118]

At another time, he says:

The use of art is to produce copies of things...without the true depiction of objects there can be no pictorial art. Nobility of sentiment and such like only come after a successful delineation of the external form of an object...He should learn to paint according to his own ideas, not slavishly copying models of old artists. Plagiarism is a crime to be avoided not only by men of letters but also by painters.[119]

In spite of these rather extreme statements, Ōkyo's work, although realistic if compared to that of his Japanese contemporaries, seems formalized and decorative if compared to the painting of the West or of Japan during the Meiji period. A good example of his style is the folding screen in the Nishimura collection in Kyoto representing the Hozu River (Plate 94). There is certainly a good deal of naturalistic detail, especially in the pines with their carefully-drawn needles and in the various leaves and grasses, and compared to the work of a Kōrin, it looks like the very height of realism. From a Western point of view, however, it seems stylized, with the space flattened out and a rather unconvincing version of water. It looks heavy and opaque, and the rocks, especially those at the right, seem almost flat. On the other

117

hand, there is a certain interest in the design, with the stream cutting a broad angle and the tree at the left balancing the rocks at the right. In fact, the appeal of his best painting lies in its decorative quality rather than in the realism on which he prided himself, and it is also rather indicative of his Japanese taste that, in spite of his study of Western perspective, the landscape as such plays a very minor role in his total work.

Among Ōkyo's many followers the most outstanding was Goshun (1752 —1811), the founder of the Shijō School. He had first studied with Buson, a leading Nanga painter, but after his master's death in 1783 he became a pupil of Ōkyo, by whom he was profoundly influenced. An example of his mature style is the winter landscape screen in the National Museum in Tokyo, which combines the realism of Ōkyo with a more poetic spirit derived from the Nanga School *(Plate 95)*. The rendering of space in depth, with the receding mountains and the tiny sails on the horizon at the upper left, indicate his interest in perspective, while the pattern of the pines and rocks and houses shows his relation to Japanese tradition. The result is a landscape which, in a minor way, expresses a mood of winter, and here, as in the companion screen of summer, the illusionistic naturalism is subordinate to the decorative qualities.

A contemporary of Goshun's who painted a much more naturalistic kind of landscape was Shiba Kōkan (1747—1818). Originally he had been a pupil of the Ukiyo-e master Harunobu, but when he saw books on Western paintings and engravings at Nagasaki he studied them and became an ardent advocate of the foreign style. His importance lies less in the intrinsic value of his paintings and engravings than in the profound influence they had on later artists, for he was the first to apply Western methods of shading and perspective systematically. He wrote extensively on the subject, and the following passage expresses his new ideals:

The style of copying nature is exemplified in Dutch pictures. Unlike our native paintings, no unnecessary ado is made about strokes, their manner, their motives, or their force. In Occidental art, objects are copied directly from nature; hence before a landscape one feels as if one were placed in the midst of nature. There is a wonderful apparatus called photograph, which gives a facsimile copy of the object, whatever it is.[120]

On another occasion, he says:

There are painters of such schools as Tosa, Kano, and Tōga (Chinese School) but they do not know how to paint Fuji in the right way. Tanyū painted Fuji many times but he could not make the picture look like the real Fuji at all. His painting is the mere play of the brush. Tōga painters are not able to create truly Japanese landscapes, they paint some imaginary mountains and lakes and call them *sansui*. They do not even tell you which Chinese mountain it is but just paint some mountain lake. It is a mere dream and nobody understands what the artist is painting ...In Western painting you find light and shadow, perspective and depth, so that it looks real and natural. In the painting of the West, things look alive and as if they could move.[121]

A typical work of Kōkan's is a colored copper engraving in the National Museum in Tokyo which represents *Shinobazu-no-Ike,* a small lake in Ueno Park *(Plate 96)*. The choice of subject itself is indicative of the new approach towards art, for the scene is taken from the everyday world surrounding the artist rather than from the imaginary world of distant China. The technique is also new, for copper engraving was a Western invention introduced to Japan by the Dutch, but the most important of all is the style, which with its diminishing shore-lines and cast shadows uses for the first time a scientific perspective and modelling. The result is a work which, though aesthetically not very rewarding, is of immense importance in the development of the Japanese landscape. It is interesting to note, however, that when Kōkan turned to painting, a more decorative quality emerged, so that this work does not resemble the Western style nearly as closely.

The two and a half centuries of the Tokugawa, or Edo, period contained a great variety of artistic styles and a number of different schools varying all the way from the highly decorative Sōtatsu School to the realistic Maruyama one, and from the traditional Kano style to the Western style of Shiba Kōkan and the *bunjinga* of the Nanga School. This diversity is the strength of the period, revealing an artistic vigor and showing, in spite of the seclusive policy of the shoguns, a surprising amount of foreign influence.

15

Landscape Painters
of the Ukiyo-e School

OF all the Japanese landscapes the most famous in the West are those of the masters of the Ukiyo-e School, especially of Hokusai and Hiroshige. In fact, for many years Japanese art was known chiefly through these artists, whose colored wood blocks have been sought by eager European and American collectors ever since they first attained general recognition at the London Exhibition of 1862 and the Paris Exposition of 1867. For a time Japanese critics tended to play down their importance in reaction to the Westerners' overestimation of them, but today there is a more balanced view of their value. As a result the Japanese themselves have come to admire and collect these masters of the woodcut, while the Westerners have learned that this last offshoot of the great artistic tradition of Japan was by no means the only contribution which the Japanese made to world art.

Ukiyo-e artists had originally portrayed the life of the gay quarters of Edo, the Yoshiwara district, painting famous beauties, geisha houses, Kabuki actors, and other phases of popular life, and it was only under the influence of Katsushika Hokusai (1760—1849) that landscape became a major subject for the artists of this school. Trained in the traditional Ukiyo-e manner by

Shunshō, who was famous for his portraits of celebrated actors, Hokusai also studied the works of the Kano and Tosa Schools, but the turning point of his career came when, through Shiba Kōkan, he discovered the style of Dutch copper engravings, from which he learned Western-type perspective.[122] Combining this new technique with native Japanese and Chinese traditions, he evolved a style which, in its originality and greatness, is perfectly expressed in his series of the thirty-six views (actually forty-six, since he added ten additional prints) of Fuji, or *Fugaku Sanjūrokukei,* now believed to have been made between 1829 and 1831. The very choice of the subject indicates the popular and truly Japanese character of *ukiyo-e,* for while Kano artists were still painting imaginary Chinese scenes Hokusai chose for his series Mount Fuji, the most sacred symbol of Japan:

In primitive times, it was believed to be a female deity of fire and later the abode of a Shintō goddess. Sometimes, it was associated with Taoist ideas, and at other times with the Buddhist faith. Today it has become the symbol of the national spirit. Its towering height inspired the Japanese to consider it the symbol of Japanese aspirations; its regular outline and graceful sweep has become the epitome of Japanese simplicity; the white snow on its summit represents the Japanese love of purity so significant in their cultural development; the soaring of Mt. Fuji above other volcanic mountains and its majesty characterizes the potential power of the Japanese people as a nation.[123]

The ancient poets of the Nara period had already celebrated the beauty of this sacred mountain, and the following poem, entitled "On a Distant View of Mount Fuji," expresses their feeling:

> Ever since heaven and earth were parted
> It has towered lofty, noble, divine,
> Mount Fuji in Suruga!
> When we look up to the plains of heaven,
> The light of the sky-traversing sun is shaded,
> The gleam of the shining moon is not seen,
> White clouds dare not cross it,
> And for ever it snows.
> We shall tell of it from mouth to mouth,
> O the lofty mountain of Fuji![124]

In his thirty-six views of Fuji, Hokusai portrays the mountain from many different angles and from a variety of different places, such as the city of Edo, the Tōkaidō, and the Koshu Kaido. The most ingenious devices are used so that the motif is ever varied. Now Fuji towers near at hand, and now it is a tiny peak in the distance. It appears above the roof tops of Edo or behind the surging waves of the sea. Sometimes the weather is clear, and sometimes it is stormy. There are views in which nothing distracts from Fuji, and there are others in which there are so many details that one hardly notices the mountain. But no matter what the scene is, Fuji is visible, an experience common to every traveller in Japan, for the mountain, rising above the other peaks, can be seen from many places.

Although the dramatic print of Fuji viewed through the waves at Kanagawa is perhaps the best known of the series, probably the most impressive is "Fuji on a Clear Day," also known as "Red Fuji," a print which has a simplicity and grandeur that makes it unique even in so wonderful a series *(Plate 97)*. Mountains had long been one of the most important elements in the landscape, but never before had a mountain so dominated the scene. Usually they loomed up in the background, but here Fuji rises directly from the front and its pyramidal shape fills almost half of the picture. Nothing distracts from the purity of its form—no mist, no streams, no fantastically-gnarled pines or rocks or figures—for everything is concentrated on the mountain. The long furrows of cloud break up the blue area of the sky just as the dotting of green breaks up the foot, so that the dark red body of the mountain stands out against the linear and the speckled patterns. A few downward streaks of snow make a contrast with the horizontal movement of the clouds and prevent the red triangle of the mountain from becoming monotonous.

Although Hokusai's complete mastery of perspective in rendering space in this series shows a Western influence, the essential character of the prints is thoroughly Japanese. Based upon an intimate knowledge of nature, the work is at the same time highly abstract and decorative, and both these qualities are very pronounced in the "Red Fuji." It is the structure of the mountain itself that the artist wishes to portray, and in this sense such a work is close to the ideals of the Post-Impressionists. They, too, were more concerned with rendering the structure of nature than with any naturalistic likeness, and it is not surprising that painters such as Van Gogh admired and even copied this great Japanese artist.

123

Another print which illustrates a different aspect of the artist's many-sided approach to Fuji is the print entitled *Fujimihara,* in which the mountain appears as a tiny peak seen through the barrel of a cooper *(Plate 98)*. Here the genre motif is dominant, and the interest is so entirely centered on the workman busy at his trade that Fuji is hardly noticeable. This emphasis on an ordinary laborer, as well as the humorous spirit in which the cooper is portrayed, is quite characteristic of Hokusai, who in his many illustrated books did thousands of scenes from daily life. In a formal sense, this print is also very different from the "Red Fuji." There is far more emphasis on space in depth, with a definite foreground, middle-ground, and background, and there is a greater use of line, especially in the figure itself and the various tools and barrel. Color, although important, is less essential than it was in the other work, and there is a use of specific detail which is completely absent in the "Red Fuji." One sees how the cloth is tied around the cooper's head, and there is even an indication of a pattern on his garment, but the detail is sparingly used, and the ground and the margin of green and the single tree are all generalized so that they do not distract from the center of interest. These two works may give some idea of the decorative as well as the humorous and narrative traits which are such important aspects, not only of Hokusai's work, but also of the Japanese tradition in painting.

There are many other landscapes in Hokusai's tremendous *oeuvre* (estimated at some thirty-five thousand pictures), but this set, which was done when he was a man of seventy, is universally regarded as his masterpiece. Among the other series the finest are the eight sheets showing a trip to celebrated waterfalls, entitled *Shokoku Takimeguri,* and published in 1827, and the eleven sheets of famous bridges from various provinces, the *Shokoku Meikio Kirai,* published between 1827 and 1830. At the age of seventy-five he returned to the theme of Mt. Fuji and made a series of one hundred black and white prints of the mountain, but none of these equal the famous thirty-six views of Fuji. Interestingly enough, during the last decade of his life he abandoned perspective and returned to the more traditional Far Eastern type of landscape with a shifting point of view and no unified space conception.

Following Hokusai, many woodcut artists, some of whom are still alive today, devoted themselves to the landscape print. By far the most distinguished

124

of these is Andō Hiroshige, whose fifty-three stages of the Tōkaidō, or *Tōkaidō Gojūsantsugi,* equals Hokusai's Fuji series in fame. Born in 1797 and dying in 1858, he was a full generation younger than Hokusai, and he is usually considered the last of the great Ukiyo-e artists. His reputation in Japan is equal to if not greater than that of the older master, although today Western critics tend to consider Hokusai the finer artist. Whatever his position, there is no doubt that he was a very original artist who made a real contribution to the art of the Japanese landscape.

The print entitled "Shower at Atake Bridge" is one of the best examples of Hiroshige's style *(Plate 99).* It shows some people who, having been caught in a sudden cloudburst, rush across the bridge trying to protect themselves from the rain. Behind them is the river where a man pushes his boat along with a pole, and beyond, the trees along the bank are dark against the grey sky. The diagonal of the bridge is repeated in the reversed diagonal of the band of trees, and there are heavy supports under the bridge which form an interesting geometric design. The color is subdued—soft greys and browns and blues—and the crosshatching of the long, slender lines of rain makes a delicate, over-all pattern. While Hokusai created dramatic and forceful prints, Hiroshige's are quieter both in their formal expression and in their mood. What interested him most was the atmospheric effect, the landscape in different seasons and in different kinds of weather, for it was not so much the underlying form of nature which fascinated him but its appearance at a given time.

Hiroshige was an extremely productive artist who over and over again portrayed the Japanese landscape in all its moods, and even today it is through his work that most Westerners see Japan. His influence has been enormous, and even people who are not familiar with his actual prints have seen reflections of his style in the work of Impressionists like Manet and Degas and, most of all, the American painter James McNeill Whistler. The latter's indebtedness to Japanese art in general and Hiroshige in particular was so profound that it might well be said that his style is unthinkable without their influence. A painting such as "Old Battersea Bridge" in the National Gallery in London is clearly derived from one of Hiroshige's compositions, and the treatment of the atmospheric effects in this and in many other works is an adaptation of what Hiroshige had done decades earlier. Whistler, like Hiroshige, was particularly fond of the muted tones of twilight and fog and dim forms seen against the sky at night, and both artists succeeded in capturing these delicate effects.

Of all Hiroshige's works the most celebrated is undoubtedly his series, published in 1834, of the stages of the Tōkaidō, the highway leading from Edo, the seat of the Tokugawa shoguns, to Kyoto, the imperial capital. There were fifty-three stations along the way, and since Hiroshige also showed the beginning at Nihonbashi and the arrival at Kyoto, there are altogether fifty-five prints in the series. Two of these may suffice to illustrate the character of the set, the first of which is a summer scene showing "Mount Fuji at Yui" *(Plate 100)*. The print is gay and colorful, with clear air and deep blue water and the white rectangle of the sails leading towards Fuji. On the cliff at the upper left there are two travellers looking out at the view, and in the center a pair of crossed pines have branches silhouetted against the sky. The effect is certainly charming but, as a view of Mount Fuji, it lacks the boldness and grandeur of the Hokusai prints.

The other scene is a winter landscape entitled "Snow at Kameyama" *(Plate 101)*. In contrast to the blues of the sea and sky in the first print, this is predominately white, with snow covering the sides of the hills and the roofs of the village at the lower left and of the castle at the extreme upper right. There are layers of snow on the bushes and trees as well as on the pine branches and their trunks, and the travellers, only partly visible as they ascend single file behind the nearest hill, are hardly noticeable beneath their large hats. The composition itself is very original, with the entire focus on the broad, slightly curving diagonal leading from the lower left corner to the upper right and leaving triangles of space in the opposite corners, which are hardly emphasized at all. The base of the diagonal is wider than the top, and its more scattered forms are balanced by the concentration of the castle and its surrounding trees. The two pines in the center are similar to those of the "Fuji at Yui" print except that, instead of the trunks crossing, they meet at an acute angle. It was this kind of unconventional composition as well as the atmospheric and tonal effects which the Impressionists admired so much in Hiroshige's work.

126

Of his many other prints which have received international acclaim, the most famous is perhaps the one called "White Rain at Shōno," which also belongs to the Tōkaidō series, and which treats the theme of figures in rain and mist in a brilliantly original manner. Another of his masterpieces, one of his views of Kyoto entitled "Cherry Blossoms at Arashiyama," expresses a more picturesque and lyrical mood. Still another aspect of his many-sided genius is illustrated in a print called "Seba," one of the sixty-nine stations of the Kisokaidō. Here, the romantic, even sentimental, side of Hiroshige comes out, a side which has a particular appeal to the Japanese.

Just as the masters of the older generation had given a wonderful picture of the world of the courtesans and the Kabuki, so Hiroshige in his thousands of landscapes portrayed the life of the late Edo period. Basing his work on what he actually saw and using a rather realistic style, his prints are, among other things, a vivid record of what Japan looked like a hundred years ago.

Hiroshige was the last great artist of the Ukiyo-e, and it is to the oil painter of the present that we must turn to conclude this study of the landscape. Some of the best-known contemporary Japanese artists have devoted themselves to landscape painting, among them Japan's most outstanding modern painter, Ryūzaburo Umehara. However, since their work is predominantly Western, it does not really form a part of the native Japanese tradition of landscape painting, and for this reason these artists will not be discussed here.

In spite of the love and even the reverence which the Japanese have always shown towards nature, it must be admitted that of the two the Chinese interpretation of the landscape is the more profound. In Japan landscape painting was most popular when the Chinese influence was strongest, and although Japanese artists such as Sesshū were able to equal and even surpass their Chinese contemporaries, most of the pure landscapes were frankly based upon Chinese models. In the native Japanese tradition the landscape played a more minor role, and when it appeared it was usually very decorative. Even Hokusai and Hiroshige, the two most original Japanese landscapists, were more interested in the formal qualities of nature than in an interpretation of nature itself, and it is perhaps in the art of the landscape gardeners and the masters of flower arrangement that the Japanese love of nature finds its fullest expression. When one thinks of the landscape painting of the Far East, it is the art of the great Sung masters which comes to mind, especially of Kuo Hsi, Mi Fei, Hsia Kuei, and Ma Yüan, for in their painting, the beauty of the natural world is deepened by the perception of something spiritual.

NOTES

1. A. Waley, *The Book of Song* (London, 1937), nos. 84 & 112.

2. J. Legge, *Confucius* ("The Chinese Classics," Vol. I [New York, 1875]), p. 35.

3. A. Waley, *The Way and Its Power* (London, 1942), p. 150.

4. *Ibid.,* p. 151.

5. A. Marcus, *Der Blaue Drache* (Zurich, 1949), p. 143.

6. C. P. Fitzgerald, *China* (Rev. ed.; New York, 1949), p. 33.

7. O. Siren, *Gardens of China* (New York, 1950), p. 451.

8. S. Sakanishi (trans.) Kuo Hsi's *An Essay on Landscape Painting* (London, 1935), p. 30.

9. Ibid., p. 31.

10. Ibid., p. 49.

11. S. Obata (trans.) *The Works of Li Po* (New York, 1922), p. 170.

12. Sakanishi, *op. cit.,* p. 38.

13. For an excellent discussion of these ideas, see G. Rowley, *Principles of Chinese Painting* (Princeton, 1947).

14. O. Siren, *The Chinese on the Art of Painting* (Peiping, 1936), p. 19.

15. Ibid., p. 71.

16. S. Sakanishi, *The Spirit of the Brush* (London, 1939), pp. 30–33.

17. A. Waley, *Introduction to Chinese Painting* (London, 1923), pp. 49–50.

18. Chang Yen-yuan, "Li Tai Ming Hua Chi" ("Records of Famous Paintings during the Various Generations"), translated in Siren, *op. cit.,* pp. 30–31.

19. O. Siren, *History of Early Chinese Painting* (London, 1933), Vol. I, Plate 9.

20. Sakanishi, *op. cit.,* p. 37.

21. A. Soper (trans.), Chu Ching-hsüan's "T'ang Ch'ao Ming Hua Lu," *Archives of the Chinese Art Society of America,* IV (1950), p. 12.

22. Siren, *Art of Painting,* pp. 30–31.

23. Soper, *op. cit.,* p. 9.

24. W. Cohn, *Chinese Painting* (London, 1948), p. 47, fig. 11.

25. *Illustrated Catalogue of Chinese Government Exhibits for the International Exhibition of Chinese Art in London* (Nanking, 1935), III, pp. 124–25.

26. S. Ise, *Ko Gaishi yori Kei Ko niitaru Shina Sansui-gwashi (A History of Chinese Landscape Painting from Ku K'ai-chih to Ching Hao)* (Tokyo, 1934), Plate II, 1–13.

27. Sakanishi, *op. cit.;* and Siren, *op. cit.,* contain translations.

28. Soper, *op. cit.,* p. 14.

29. B. Laufer, "The Wang Ch'uan Tu, A Landscape by Wang Wei," *Ostasiatische Zeitschrift,* Alte Folge Vol. I, pp. 28–55.

30. *Ibid.,* p. 30.

31. Siren, *Early Painting,* Vol. I, Plates 53–56.

32. Another Ming copy after this artist by Chao Tso is mentioned by Siren in his *History of Later Chinese Painting,* I, p. 188.

33. L. Bachhofer, Chinesische Landschaftsmalerei vom X-XIII, Jahrundert, *Sinica* X. Jahrgang (Frankfurt, 1935), No. I, pp. 15–16.

34. Siren, *Early Painting,* Vol. I, Plate 25.

35. Tōyei Shūko, *An Illustrated Catalogue of the Ancient Imperial Treasury called Shōsō-in* (Tokyo, 1926–27), Vol. III, Plates 171 a, b; and Vol. V, Plates 282, 293 a, b; and 294 a, b.

36. A. Soper (trans.), Kuo Jo-hsü's *Experiences in Painting* (Washington, 1951).

37. L. Bachhofer, "Die Raumdarstellung in der Chinesischen Malerei des ersten Jahrtausends n. Chr.," *Münchner Jahrbuch der Bildenden Kunst,* Band VIII (1931), pp. 193–242.

38. Sakanishi, *op. cit.,* p. 90.

39. Siren, *op. cit.,* Plate 89.

40. Soper, *op. cit.,* p. 17.

41. *Ibid.*, p. 136.

42. Siren, *op. cit.*, Plate 89A; or Harada, *Pageant of Chinese Painting* (Tokyo, 1936), Plate 23.

43. Soper, *op. cit.*, p. 46.

44. Sakanishi, *op. cit.*, p. 79.

45. *Ibid.*, p. 79.

46. Soper, *op. cit.*, p. 159.

47. *Ibid.*, p. 158.

48. H. A. Giles, *An Introduction to Chinese Pictorial Art* (London, 1918), p. 99.

49. Soper, *op. cit.*, p. 46.

50. *Ibid.*, pp. 60–61.

51. *Ibid.*, p. 175.

52. O. Siren, *Kinas Konst Under Tre Artusenden* (Stockholm, 1943), fig. 270; or Harada, *op. cit.*, Plate 56.

53. Soper, *op. cit.*, p. 171.

54. R. Torii, *Culture of the Liao Dynasty* ("Illustrations of Archaeology," Vol. II [Tokyo, 1936]), Plates 205–07; or *Kokka*, No. 491 (October, 1931); and most recently, J. Tamura and Y. Kobayashi, *Tombs and Mural Paintings of Ch'ing Ling* (Kyoto, 1952).

55. Siren, *Early Painting,* Vol. I, Plate 64.

56. Soper, *op. cit.*, p. 60.

57. Sakanishi, *An Essay . . .,* p. 38.

58. *Ibid.*, p. 31.

59. Siren, *op. cit.*, Vol. II, Plates 1–2.

60. Cohn, *op. cit.*, Plate 56.

61. *Ibid.*, Plates 58–59.

62. *Ibid.*, Plates 70–72.

63. S. Shimada, "On the Landscape Paintings in the Kōtō-in, Kyoto, *Bijutsu Kenkyu,* No. CLXV, Vol. IV (1951).

64. *Ibid.*, Plates VI and VII.

65. Cohn, *op. cit.*, Plate 68.

66. For a colored reproduction of the entire scroll, see O. Siren, *Chinese Paintings in the Bahr Collection* (London, 1938), Plate XI.

67. W. Speiser, *Meisterwerke Chinesischer Malerei aus der Sammlung der Japanischen Reichsmarschälle Yoshimitsu and Yoshimasa* (Berlin, 1947).

68. Siren, *Early Painting*, Vol. II, p. 84.

69. *Ibid.*, Plate 59; and Cohn, *op. cit.*, Plate 92.

70. Siren, *op. cit.*, Plates 64–66.

71. Cohn, *op. cit.*, Plates 94–96; and *Cat. of Chin. London Exhib.*, pp. 88–97.

72. Cohn, *op. cit.*, Plate 104.

73. *Ibid.*, Plate 100.

74. Speiser, *op. cit.*, p. 12.

75. Cohn, *op. cit.*, Plate 107; and Siren, *op. cit.*, Vol. II, Plate 83.

76. W. Speiser, "Die Yüan Klassik der Landschaftsmalerei," *Ostasiatische Zeitschrift* Neue Folge VII, Heft 1; also Speiser, "Landschafter der Yüan Zeit," *Sinica*, XI (1936).

77. Siren, *Art of Painting*, p. 122.

78. B. March, *Some Technical Terms of Chinese Painting* (Baltimore, 1938), p. 19; for comparison, see Cohn, *op. cit.*, Plate 154; and Siren, *Early Painting*, Vol. II, Plate 118.

79. Giles, *op. cit.*, p. 160.

80. Waley, *op. cit.*, p. 248.

81. Siren, *History of Later Chinese Painting* (London, 1938), Vol. II; and V. Contag, *Die Sechs berümten Maler der Ch'ing Dynastie* (Munich, 1940).

82. *Cat. of Chin. London Exhib.*, pp. 143–47.

83. Translated in V. Contag, *Die beiden Steine* (Brunswick, 1950); also in part in Siren, *Art of Painting*.

84. *The Manyōshū* (Nippon Gakujitsu Shinkōkai ed.; Tokyo, 1940), p. 182.

85. *Ibid.*, p. 172.

86. Waley, *op. cit.*, p. 134 and Plate XXVI.

87. *Japanese Art* ("Sekai Bijitsu Zenshū," Vol. I [Tokyo, 1952]), Color Plate 9.

88. N. Tsuda, *Handbook of Japanese Art* (Tokyo, 1935), p. 460.

89. O. Kümmel, *Die Kunst Chinas und Japans* (Potsdam, 1929), pp.

65 and 124.

90. A. Soper, "The Rise of Yamato-e," *The Art Bulletin,* XXIV (December, 1942), p. 355.

91. Color reproduction may be seen in *Tōyō Bijitsu Taikwan* (Tokyo, 1909), Vol. I, Plate 8.

92. S. Taki, *Japanese Fine Arts* (Tokyo, 1931), p. 113.

93. Color reproduction may be seen in *Geienjuhō,* Vol. II, (Kyoto, 1943), Plate 71.

94. H. Minamoto, *An Illustrated History of Japanese Art* (Kyoto, 1935), Plate 77.

95. K. Toda, *Japanese Scroll Painting* (Chicago, 1935), p. 14.

96. *Ibid.,* p. 15.

97. *Tōyō Bijitsu Taikwan,* Vol. I, Plate 48.

98. Minamoto, *op. cit.,* Plate 106.

99. *Ibid.,* Plate 105.

100. T. Akiyama, "Senzui Byōbu Owned by the Jingo-ji," *Bijitsu Kenkyu,* October, 1941.

101. Color reproduction may be seen in *Geienjuhō, op. cit.,* Plate 21.

102. S. Omura, *History of Japanese Pictorial Art* (Tokyo, 1909), p. 82.

103. *Pageant of Japanese Art,* (Tokyo, 1952), Vol. II, Plate 52.

104. *Ibid.,* Plate 53.

105. *Ibid.,* Plate 54.

106. J. C. Covell, *Under the Seal of Sesshū* (New York, 1941), p. 7.

107. For discussion of the inscription, *ibid.,* p. 83.

108. S. Tajima, *Masterpieces of Motonobu* (Tokyo, 1904), Vol. I, introduction.

109. *Ibid.,* for reproduction of complete set.

110. *Pageant . . ., op. cit.,* Plate 66.

111. Color reproduction may be seen in H. Okuhira, *E no Rekishi, Nihon* (Tokyo, 1943), Vol. II, Plate 1.

112. Color reproduction, *ibid.,* Plate 6.

113. N. Tsuda, *Ideals of Japanese Painting* (Tokyo, 1940), fig. 29.

114. *Japanese Art* ("University Prints," [Newton, 1940]), Plate 0376.

115. *Japanese Art* ("Sekai Bijitsu Zenshū," Vol. III), Color Plate 14.

116. R. Paine, "Landscapes and Figures," *Catalogue of a Special Exhibition of Japanese Screen Painting in the Boston Museum of Fine Arts* (Boston, 1938), Plate 21.

117. Color reproduction may be seen in *Pageant . . ., op. cit.,* Plate 87.

118. L. Binyon, *The Flight of the Dragon* (London, 1911), p. 102.

119. *Ibid.,* p. 103.

120. *Ibid.,* p. 101.

121. M. Seki, *Dai Nippon Kaigashi* (Tokyo, 1934), p. 396.

122. For an example of a Western-style work by Hokusai, see *Pageant . . ., op. cit.,* p. 91.

123. Tsuda, *op. cit.,* p. 65.

124. *Manyōshū, op. cit.,* p. 187.

BIBLIOGRAPHY

WORKS ON CHINESE LANDSCAPE PAINTING

L. Bachhofer. "Chinesisiche Landschaftsmalerei," vom X-XIII, Jahrundert, *Sinica,* X, 1–2.

E. Dietz. *Shan Shui.* Vienna, 1943.

O. Fischer. *Chinesische Landschaftsmalerei* (Rev. ed.), Berlin, 1943.

S. Ise. *Ko Gaishi yori Kei Ko niitaru Shina Sansui-gwashi.* Tokyo, 1934.

A. Salmony. *Chinesische Landschaftsmalerei.* Berlin, 1921.

A. Soper. "Early Chinese Landscape Painting," *Art Bulletin,* (June, 1941).

W. Speiser. "Die Yuan Klassik der Landschaftsmalerei, *Ostasiatische Zeitschrift,* N. F. VII, 1.

TRANSLATIONS OF CHINESE TEXTS ON PAINTING

V. Contag. *Die Beiden Steine.* Brunswick, 1950.

S. Sakanishi. *An Essay on Landscape Painting* (Kuo Hsi). London, 1935.

——. *The Spirit of the Brush.* London, 1939.

O. Siren. *The Chinese on the Art of Painting.* Peiping, 1936.

A. Soper. "T'ang Ch'ao Ming Hua Lu" (Chu Ching-hsüan), *Archives of the Chinese Art Society of America* (New York), IV (1950).

——. *Kuo Jo-hsü's Experiences in Painting.* Washington, 1951.

GENERAL BOOKS ON CHINESE PAINTING

L. Binyon. *Painting in the Far East* (Rev. ed.), London, 1934.

W. Cohn. *Chinese Painting.* London, 1948.

J. C. Ferguson. *Chinese Painting*. Chicago, 1927.

H. A. Giles. *Introduction to the History of Chinese Pictorial Art*. London, 1918.

E. Grosse. *Ostasiatische Tuschmalerei*. Berlin, 1923.

F. Hirth. *Scraps from a Collector's Notebook*. Leiden, 1905.

B. March. *Some Technical Terms of Chinese Painting*. Baltimore, 1935.

G. Rowley. *Principles of Chinese Painting*. Princeton, 1947.

O. Siren. *History of Early Chinese Painting*. London, 1933.

———. *History of Later Chinese Painting*. London, 1938.

W. Speiser. *Meisterwerke Chinesischer Malerei*. Berlin, 1947.

A. Waley. *Introduction to the Study of Chinese Painting*. London, 1923.

COLLECTIONS OF REPRODUCTIONS OF
CHINESE PAINTINGS

M. Akiyama. *Sōgen Meigwa Shū*. Tokyo, 1930.

L. Binyon. *Chinese Paintings in English Collections*. London, 1927.

E. Chavannes and R. Petrucci. *La Peinture Chinoise au Musee Cernuschi*. Paris, 1914.

L. Hackney and Yau Chang-foo. *A Study of Chinese Painting in the Moore Collection*. New York, 1940.

B. Harada. *A Pageant of Chinese Painting*. Tokyo, 1936.

Illustrated Catalogue of the Chinese Government Exhibition of Chinese Art in London, Vol. III. Nanking, 1935.

Kokka. Tokyo, monthly since 1889.

Ku Kung Shu Hua Chi, Vols. I-XLV. Peiping, 1930 ff.

O. Siren. *Chinese Paintings in American Collections*. London, 1927.

———. *Early Chinese Paintings from the Bahr Collection*. London, 1938.

K. Tomita. *Portfolio of Chinese Paintings in the Museum of Fine Arts*. Boston, 1938.

S. Tajima. *Nansō Meigaen*. Tokyo, 1908–13.

Tōsō Genmin Meigwa Taikwan. Tokyo, 1928.

Tōyō Bijitsu Taikwan, Vols. VII-XII. Tokyo, 1908 ff.

WORKS ON JAPANESE PAINTING

W. Anderson. *The Pictorial Arts of Japan.* London, 1886.

L. Binyon. *Painting in the Far East* (4th ed.), London, 1934.

H. P. Bowie. *On the Laws of Japanese Painting.* San Francisco, 1911.

W. Cohn. *Stilanalysen als Einführung in die Japanische Malerei.* Berlin, 1908.

J. C. Covell. *Under the Seal of Sesshū.* New York, 1941.

S. Elisséeff. *La Peinture Contemporaine au Japon.* Paris, 1923.

E. Grosse. *Die Ostasiatische Tuschmalerei.* Berlin, 1922.

H. Minamoto. *An Illustrated History of Japanese Art.* Kyoto, 1935.

A. Morrison. *The Painters of Japan.* London, 1911.

S. Omura. *History of Japanese Pictorial Art.* Tokyo, 1909.

Pageant of Japanese Art, Vols. I-II. Tokyo, 1952.

R. Paine. *Ten Japanese Paintings.* New York, 1939.

A. Soper. "The Rise of Yamato-e," *Art Bulletin,* XXIV (1942).

K. Toda. *Japanese Scroll Painting.* Chicago, 1935.

N. Tsuda. *Ideals of Japanese Painting.* Tokyo, 1940.

Y. Yashiro. *Japanische Malerei der Gegenwart.* Berlin, 1931.

BOOKS ON JAPANESE PRINTS

O. Benesch. *Die Spätmeister des Japanischen Holzschitts.* Vienna, 1938.

L. Binyon. *Japanese Color Prints.* London, 1923.

E. d. Goncourt. *Hokusai.* Paris, 1896.

J. Kurth. *Die Geschichte des Japanischen Holzschitts,* 3 vols. Leipzig, 1925.

M. Narazaki and I. Kondō. *Nippon Fūkei Hangashi-ron.* Tokyo, 1943.

Y. Noguchi. *Hiroshige.* Tokyo, 1934.

——. *Hiroshige and Japanese Landscapes.* Tokyo, 1934.

——. *Hokusai.* London, 1925.

W. v. Seidlitz. *History of Japanese Color Prints.* London, 1920.

E. Strange. *Color Prints of Hiroshige.* London, 1925.

COLLECTIONS OF REPRODUCTIONS OF
JAPANESE PAINTINGS

Catalogue of the Exhibition of Japanese Painting and Sculpture sponsored by the Government of Japan. Washington, 1953.

Geienjuhō, Vol. II. Kyoto, 1953.

Katalog der Ausstellung Altjapanischer Kunst. Berlin, 1939.

Kokka. Tokyo, monthly since 1889.

Nihon-ga Taisei, 28 vols. Tokyo, 1931.

H. Okuhira. *E no Rekishi, Nihon,* Vols. I-II. Tokyo, 1953.

R. Paine. *Catalogue of a Special Exhibition of Japanese Screen Painting; Birds and Animals.* Boston 1935.

———. *Catalogue of a Special Exhibition of Japanese Screen Paintings; Landscapes and Figures.* Boston, 1938.

Sekai Bijitsu Zenshū, Vols. I-III, "Japanese Art." Tokyo, 1952.

S. Tajima. *Masterpieces of Motonobu.* Tokyo, 1904.

———. *Shimbi Taikwan,* 20 vols. Tokyo, 1899–1908.

Tōyō Bijitsu Taikwan, Vols, I-VI. Tokyo, 1932 ff.

Ukiyo-e Taikashūsei, 26 vols. Tokyo, 1932.

University Prints, "Japanese Art." Newton, 1940.

138

INDEX

Abe collection, 36
Abstract, 62, 83, 100, 112, 113, 116
Academic painters, 71, 74
Academic school, 71
Academicism, 9, 10
"Admonitions of the Imperial Preceptress," 14
Aerial perspective, 34, 44
Album leaf, 54, 56
American collections, 52, 54, 56, 121
Ashikaga period, 48, 52, 95, 106
Asuka period, 83
Atmosphere, 27, 28, 29, 32, 33, 34, 37, 38, 40,
    91, 97, 125, 126
Attribution, 22
Authenticity of paintings, 9, 28, 32, 38
"Autumn Day in the Valley of the Yellow
    River," 44
"Autumn River Landscape," 68
Azuchi, 105–6

Bachhofer, 32
Bahr collection, 27
Bamboo, 5, 83
Bayen, 97
"Big Fool," 61
Biwa, 29, 85
Blue and green, 20, 21, 24, 27, 29, 48–49
"Boneless painting," 27
Boston Museum, 17, 22, 35, 38, 41, 48, 54, 55,
    56, 114
British Museum, 14
"Broken-ink," 62
Brushwork, 20, 21, 24, 27, 33, 34, 36, 47, 67,
    68, 75, 76, 99, 100, 116
Buddha, 57, 83
Buddhism, 5, 82, 92, 122
Buddhist caves, 28
Buddhist legend, 16, 28
Buddhist painting, 16, 20, 24, 31, 84, 88, 89
Buddhist priest, 37
"Buddhist Temple," 36
Bunjinga, 115, 119
Buson, 116, 118
Byōbu, 91, 105

Byōdō-in, 88

Calligrapher, 14, 45, 66, 100
Calligraphy, 11, 71, 116
Catalogue of the Imperial Collection, 35, 37, 40
Catalogue of Yoshimasa collection, 95
"Cave of the Immortals," 39
Cézanne, 59, 60
Ch'an Buddhism, 5, 56, 57, 58
Ch'an painting, 57–58
Chang Yen-yüan, 14, 15, 20, 32
Chao Po-chü, 46, 48, 49, 51, 70, 72
Chao Ta-nien, 71
Chê School, 66, 68, 70
Chêkiang, 66
"Cherry Blossoms at Arashiyama," 127
Ch'i-yün shêng-tung, 10, 74
Chiang Kuan-tao, 71
Ch'ien Lung, 73
Ch'iu Ch'êng Palace, 22
Ch'in Ting P'ei Wên Chai Shu Hua P'u, 73
Ch'iu Ying, 48, 70–71
Chinese critics, 36, 60, 66, 74
Chinese collections, 64
Chinese ideals, 96, 115
Chinese influence, 82–86, 90–91, 95–96, 97–98,
    101, 103, 115, 127
Chinese poets, 82
Chinese scholars, 51
Chinese subjects, 101, 112, 113
Chinese thought, 60
Ch'ing critics, 31
Ching Hao, 33–34, 35, 37
Ch'ing lü pai, 48
Ch'ing lü shan shui, 21
Ch'ing painting, 6, 9, 116
Ch'ing period, 52, 60, 73–74
Chinkai, 88
Chion-in, 70
Chō Denso, 96
Chōgosonshi-ji, 90
Chou period, 4
Chu Ching-hsüan, 20, 21, 24
Chü-jan, 37, 40–41, 66, 74

139

Chü-jen, 6
Chu Ta, 76
Cincinnati Art Museum, 54
"Clear Day in the Valley," 38
"Clearing after Snowfall," 26
Cleveland Museum, 46
Clouds, 22, 27, 29, 32, 33, 37, 45
"Cloud-Terrace Mountain," 14
Colored painting, 20, 21, 23, 25, 27, 29, 46,
    48–49, 70, 77, 85, 88, 92, 102
Communists, 78
Confucian scenes, 17
Confucius, 4, 5, 10, 60
Courbet, 9
Court artists, 66

Daigo-ji, 84
Daily life, 65, 67
Daisen-in, 101
Daitoku-ji, 101
Decorative, 88, 90, 92, 102, 106, 109, 113,
    117–8, 124
Deer-park scrolls, 42
Degas, 125
Depth, 32, 34, 35, 91, 97
Detroit Art Institute, 64
Dhyani, 56
Dragons, 4, 14, 33
"Dry-brush painting," 63
Dutch painting, 55, 118–9

Early Ch'ing period, 73
Eclecticism, 10, 71, 73, 74, 76
Edo period, 102, 103, 111
"Eight Views," 7–8, 57, 58, 96, 112
E-makimono, 84, 88, 89
Engraving, 118, 119
Esoteric sects, 89
"Essay on Landscape Painting," 6, 43
Expressionistic, 68, 76

Famous Painters of the T'ang Dynasty, 20
Fan K'uan, 34, 41–42, 44, 53, 74
Fifth Sesshu, 108
"Fifty-Three Stages of the Tōkaidō," 126
Figures, 13, 15, 28, 29
Figure painting, 13, 20, 29, 57, 59
Filial piety, 17
Fishermen, 6, 8, 55, 67, 68
Five Dynasties period, 28, 31, 42
Fog, 32, 37, 126
Forgeries, 23
"Four Sages of Shang Shan," 54
Four Wangs, 73, 74
Freer Gallery, 15, 26, 27, 33, 41, 44, 45, 46,
    55, 62, 67, 68, 69, 74, 77, 113
Fu-ch'un mountains, 61, 74

Fugaku Sanjūrokukei, 122
Fuji prints 122–4; see also Mt. Fuji
"Fuji on a Clear Day," 123
Fujita collection, 89
Fujiwara collection, 97
Fujiwara period, 88, 106
Fusuma, 105, 106

Gay quarters, 121
Geiami, 100
Geisha, 121
General Li, 19, 21
Genji Monogatari, 112, 113
Genji Monogatari scroll, 88, 107
Genre, 90, 124
Gentleman-painter, 6, 11, 27, 60, 66, 69
"Gentlemen's painting," 115
Giotto, 15
Gold, 29, 114
Gold leaf, 105
Gold outlines, 24, 48–49
Golden Girdle, 52, 53
Golden Pavilion, 95
Goshun, 118
Gyokukan, 100

Han dynasty, 48
"Han Emperor," 48
Han period, 11, 13
Harunobu, 118
Hasegawa School, 108
Hawks and pines screen, 106, 108
Heian period, 87–88
Hermits, 6–7, 60, 62, 66, 67, 89
Hideyoshi, 105, 106
Hiroshige, 121, 125, 126, 127
History of Painting, 45
Hōgen En-i, 91
Hokusai, 121–4, 126
Hōraisan, 96
Hōryū-ji, 83
Hsia Kuei, 47, 51, 52, 55–56, 58, 66, 97, 99,
    100, 101, 102, 128
Hsiao and Hsiang Rivers, 7–8, 57, 58, 71, 96,
    112
Hsieh Ho, 10, 74
Hsien-tsung, 88
Hsü Pên, 63
Hsüan Ho Hua P'u, 35
Hua Mountains, 60
Hua Yü Lu, 75
Hua Yün-t'ai Shan Chi, 14
Huang Kung-wang, 60–62, 64, 74
Hui Tsung, 11, 34, 35, 37, 40, 46, 48, 51

Ieyasu, 111
Imperial Academy of Painting, 43, 51, 52, 53

Imperial collection, 14, 34
Imperial court, 16, 47
Imperial Encyclopedia of Calligraphy and Painting, 73
Impressionists, 8, 125
Ippen Shōnin Eden, 91
"Iron Pagoda," 89
Ise shrine, 81
Ink washes, 39, 45
"Introduction to Landscape Painting," 15
Italian Primitives, 15
Itsukushima scroll, 107
Iwasaki collection, 55

Japanese artistic tradition, 106
Japanese collections, 52, 56, 57, 58
Japanese critics, 106
Japanese poetry, 81–82
Japanese print-makers, 53
Japanese scholars, 52, 84
Japanese-style painters, 88
Japanese subjects, 102
Jataka scenes, 16, 83
Jingo-ji, 91
Jōgan Period, 87
Josetsu, 96, 97
Jū Ben Jū Gi, 115
Jukō-in, 106

Kabuki, 121
Kakei, 97
Kakemono, 91, 92
Kako Genzai Inga Kyō, 83
Kambachi, 29
Kamakura period, 90
K'an pi, 63
K'ang Hsi, 73
Kangikō-ji, 91
Kanjō, 89
Kano Eitoku, 105–7, 108, 112
Kano Masanobu, 111
Kano Motonobu, 101–2, 105, 111, 112
Kano Naonobu, 112
Kano School, 101–2, 106, 108, 111, 113, 115, 117, 119, 122
Kano Tanyū, 112–3, 119
Kao K'o-kung, 63–64
Kao Tsung, 48
Kasuga *mandara*, 92
Kasuga Shrine, 92
Kawabata collection, 115
Kinkaku-ji, 95
Kintaikan Sayūchōki, 95
Kisokaidō, 127
Kōbō Daishi, 88
Komor collection, 61, 77
Konchi-in, 48, 96

Korea, 97
Korean, 83
Kōrin, 114–5, 117
Koseno Kanaoka, 87, 92
Kōshū Kaidō, 123
Kudara no Kawanari, 87
Kümmel, 85
Kōtō-in, 47
Ku hua, 27
Ku K'ai-chih, 14–15, 16
Kuan Chung, 48
"K'uan-lun Mountains," 33
Kuan Tsung, 52
Kuan T'ung, 34, 35, 41
Kublai Khan, 63
Kumano shrines, 92
Kung pi, 20, 49
Kuo Chung-shu, 25
Kuo Hsi, 6–10, 43–44, 47, 49, 63, 66, 76, 97, 128
Kuo Jo-hsü, 32, 34, 35, 37, 43
Kuon-ji, 48
Kuroda collection, 53
Kyōōgokoku-ji, 88

Lacquer objects, 85, 107
Lake Biwa, 105
Lake Tung-t'ing, 8
Lao-tzu, 4, 10
Late Ming period, 72
Li Chao-tao, 21–24, 25, 29
Li Ch'êng, 35–36, 41, 72, 74
Li Jen Hsing, 24
Li Po, 7, 8
Li Ssu-hsün, 19–20, 21, 23, 26, 37, 48, 77
Li T'ang, 46, 47–48, 49, 51, 53, 68, 69, 99
"Literary men's painting," 52
Li Tsung, 52
Liang K'ai, 57, 108
Liao tomb, 42, 90
"Life-movement," 10
"Life spirit," 74
Light and dark, 61, 64, 68, 75
Lin Ch'üan Kao Chih, 43
Lo Chên-yü collection, 26
Lo-yang Mansion, 23
"Lofty Message of Forests and Streams," 43
London National Gallery, 125

Ma family, 53
Ma Ho-chih, 72
Makimono, 99
Manchu dynasty, 73, 115
Mandara, 92
Manet, 125
Manyōshū, 81–82
Marin, 57

Maruyama Ōkyo, 117–8
Maruyama School, 117, 119
Marxists, 78
Matsudaira collection, 57
Matsushima, 113, 114
Ma Yüan, 47, 48, 51, 52–55, 58, 65, 66, 68, 97, 99, 101, 102
Meiji period, 117
Memorial stele, 36
Mêng-fu, 72
Metropolitan Museum, 27, 46, 49, 62
Mi Fei, 19, 33, 34, 35, 36, 37, 41, 44, 49, 53, 63, 64, 66
Mikasa hills, 92
Minchō, 96
Ming critic, 38
Ming emperor, 101
Ming Huang, 20, 21
Ming painting, 98, 101, 113,
Ming period, 6, 9, 25, 51, 65, 66, 115
Ming rulers, 65
Ming scholars, 26, 33, 48
Mirrors, 13, 29, 85
Mist, 7, 24, 33, 37, 41, 45
Mitsui collection, 54
Mi Yu-jên, 45
Modern art, 75
Modern critics, 38
Modern scholars, 27, 52
Mokkei, 101, 108
Momoyama, 105
Mongolia, 32, 42, 90
Monks, 57, 58; see also Zen priests
Monochrome, 25, 31, 37, 51, 85, 92, 93
Moore, H., 62
Mōri collection, 99
Mountains, 4, 6, 8, 13, 15, 22, 23, 25, 26, 28, 29, 33, 34, 41, 43, 46, 61, 83, 84, 86, 119
Mt. Fuji, 113, 119, 122–6
Mt. Minobu, 48
Mu-ch'i, 58, 101
Muromachi period, 95–103
Myōshin-ji, 102
Mysticism, 5, 8, 57

Nachi Waterfall, 92
Nakamura collection, 45
Nanga, 100, 103, 115–7, 118
Nara period, 81, 86, 103, 122
Narrative, 68, 71, 88, 90, 99
Nelson Gallery, 17, 36, 42, 55, 76
Neo-Confucianism, 113
Nezu collection, 92
Nishimura collection, 117
Ni Tsan, 62, 63, 65, 67, 74, 116
Ning Tsung, 53
Nōami, 100

Nobunaga, 105
Nomura collection, 102
Northern capital, 46
Northern School, 26, 48, 52, 66, 70, 76, 77, 100
Northern Sung painters, 63, 66
Northern Sung period, 45, 46, 49, 51
"Notes on Brushwork," 33
"Nymph of Lo River," 15

Ogawa collection, 24, 26
Ohara collection, 91
"Old Battersea Bridge," 125
Oracle bones, 3
Osaka Museum, 36

Pa-ta Shan-jên, 76
Painter's manual, 10
Painter-scholar, 9
Palin, 32, 42
Pantheism, 53
Peking National Museum, 21, 56
Peking Palace Museum, 23, 24, 28, 31, 33, 34, 39, 40, 41, 42, 44, 45, 56, 74, 85
P'en Lai Shan, 96
Perspective, 17, 119
Philosophy, 4, 56
Pines, 5, 114, 117
P'ang Lai-ch'ên collection, 61
Plectrum guards, 85
P'o mo, 57, 62
Poets, 24, 66, 70
"Poet on a Mountain," 67
Political art, 78
Post-Impressionists, 123
Poussin, 32
"Priest Ling-yün Viewing Peach Blossoms," 101
Professionals, 60, 66
Professional painters, 52

Rain, 125
Realism, 9, 32, 102, 117–8
Realistic, 67
Realistic detail, 65
"Red Fuji," 123, 124
Reiun-in, 102
Religious ceremony, 89
Religious painting, 92
Rembrandt, 55
Renaissance, 71
"Rivers and Hills in Wind and Rain," 38
River scene, 68
Rocks, 6, 20, 29
Romantic, 53, 67
Rubbings, 20, 25
Ryōshin, 98

Sage, 6, 8, 53
"Sages in a Landscape," 77
"Sailboat in the Rain," 56
Saigyō Monogatari, 91
San-ami, 100
Sakyamuni, 83, 84
Scholars, 5, 66, 69
School of painting, 96
Screens, 29, 85, 89, 105, 106, 107
Seal, 22, 23, 45
Seasons, 9, 35, 42, 47, 91, 112
"Seba," 127
Seikadō, 113
"Secrets of Landscape Painting," 35
Seiryō-den, 87
Senzui byōbu, 89, 91
Sesshū, 95, 98–100, 102, 103, 108, 109, 127
Sesshū School, 112
Sesson, 102–3
Shading, 38
Shadows, 119
Shan-jên, 60
Shan shui, 4
Shan Shui Chüeh, 35
Shan Shui Sü, 15
Shang, 3
Shên Chou, 67, 68, 69, 70, 98
Shên Kua, 37
Shiba Kōkan, 118–9
Shigisan Engi scroll, 89
Shih-erh Chang, 4
Shih Ching, 3
Shih-t'ao, 6, 75, 116
Shijō School, 118
Shin manner, 100
Shingon, 89
Shinobazu-no-Ike, 119
Shintō, 122
Shintoism, 81
Shinto thought, 92
Shōhekiga, 105
Shōji, 105
Shōkoku-ji, 97, 98
Shōkoku Meikio Kirai, 124
Shōkoku Takimeguri, 124
Shōmu, 84
Sho-sho-hakkei, 96
"Shower at Atake Bridge," 125
Shūbun, 97, 98, 103
Shunsō, 122
Shōsō-in, 21, 28, 82, 84–86
"Side-horned" design, 53
Silver, 29
Six canons, 10
Six Dynasties period, 14
Snow, 26, 126
"Snow at Kameyama," 126

Sōami, 95, 100–1
Sōtatsu, 113–4
Sōtatsu School, 90, 113, 116, 119
Southern capital, 14, 57
Southern School, 24, 25, 27, 45, 52, 60, 66, 67, 76, 115
Southern Sung, 51, 52, 56
Southern Sung Academy, 70
Southern Sung capital, 98
Southern Sung painting, 96, 97–98, 101, 112
Space, 17, 23, 27, 28, 29, 32, 33, 34, 36, 37, 44, 68, 83, 85, 89, 91, 92, 97, 99, 107
"Spirit-resonance," 10
"Splashed-ink," 57, 100
"Spring Morning at the Palace of the Han Emperors," 49
Stone engraving, 25
Storm, 69, 102
Su Tung-po, 19
Suiboku, 96, 97, 102, 106, 108
Suijaku, 92
Sumi, 97
Sumiyoshi School, 88
Sun Goddess, 81
"Sutra of the Past and Present Karma," 83
Symbolic, 13

Ta-ch'in, 61
Tai Chin, 68–69, 70, 98
Taiga, 115–6
Taizō-in, 96
"Tale of Genji" scroll, 88
Tamamushi Shrine, 83, 84
T'ang court, 85
T'ang critics, 14, 20, 32
T'ang emperors, 22
T'ang painting, 59, 65
T'ang period, 9, 11, 19–29
T'ang Yin, 69, 70
Tao, 4, 5, 8, 16, 39, 56
Tao-chi, 75
Taoists, 60, 78
Tao-jên, 60
Taoist inspiration, 16
Taoist landscape, 14, 53
Taoist monks, 75
Taoist painting, 31
Tao Tê Ching, 4
Tea ceremony, 95, 106
Teahouse, 107
Tea master, 100
"Ten Conveniences and Ten Enjoyments," 115
"Thirty-Six Views of Fuji," 122
Tien, 38
Tien-t'ung Shan, 98
Tōdai-ji, 84
Tōga School, 119

Tōhaku, 107, 108
Tō-ji, 88, 91
Tōkaidō Gojūsantsugi, 125
Tōkaidō, 123, 125
Tokonoma, 107
Tokugawa period, 101
Tokugawa shogunate, 111, 113, 126
Tokyo National Museum, 54, 57, 97, 100, 113, 118, 119
Tokyo University of Arts, 106
Tosa Mitsunobu, 101
Tosa School, 88, 112, 119, 122
"Travellers in Mountain Landscape," 85
Trees, 5–6, 13, 15, 22, 23, 25, 26, 27, 29, 33, 34, 35, 36, 47, 61, 70, 72
"Tribute Horse," 46
Tsugaru collection, 114
Ts'un, 38
Tsung Ping, 15, 16
Tu Fu, 7, 24
Tun Huang, 16, 28, 32, 84
Tung Ch'i-ch'ang, 19, 26, 33, 38, 66, 71, 74
Tung Yüan, 37–40, 53, 55, 66, 71, 72, 74

Uji-bashi, 107
Uji River, 107
Ukiyo-e, 90, 103, 115, 118, 121–7
Umehara, 127
Unkoku School, 109
Unkoku Tōgan, 109

Van Gogh, 123

Wang Cheng-kuo, 77
Wang Chi-ch'üan, 77
Wang Chien, 74
Wang Ch'uan, 24, 25
Wang Hui, 74, 75, 76, 77
Wang Li, 60
Wang Mêng, 61–62, 74
Wang River, 25
Wang Shih-min, 74
Wang Wei, 24–28, 67, 74
Wang Yüan-ch'i, 74
Water buffalo, 47

Waterfalls, 6, 124
Wên Chêng-ming, 70, 71
Wên jên hua, 52, 66, 67, 115
West Lake, 57
Western art, 5, 7, 11, 32, 59, 117–9
Western artists, 57
Western critics, 60, 73
Western perspective, 77, 117–8, 122, 123
Western scholars, 58
Western-style art, 78
Wet-ink, 37
Whistler, 54, 125–126
"White Rain at Shōno," 127
Willows, 6, 15, 23, 54, 72, 107
Winter landscape, 26, 28, 31, 35, 47, 57
Woodcut, 121, 124
Wu Chên, 67, 74
Wu-hsien, 66
Wu School, 66, 67, 69, 70
Wu Tao-tzu, 19, 20–21, 47

Yamaguchi collection, 116
Yamato-e, 88, 90, 91, 101, 103, 106, 113
Yang Shêng, 27
Yangtze River, 41
Yellow River, 8
Ying Yü-Chien, 57, 58, 100, 102, 112
Yoshikawa collection, 57
Yoshimasa, 57, 95, 100
Yoshimitsu, 52, 95
Yoshimochi, 97
Yoshiwara district, 121
Yüan Chiang, 76
Yüan critics, 31
Yüan painters, 36, 66
Yüan painting, 40, 95, 98
Yüan period, 9, 27, 32, 59
Yüan scholars, 48
Yumedono Kannon, 84
Yūshō, 108

Zen, 5, 56, 95, 98
Zen monasteries, 96, 102
Zen priests, 93, 95–96, 97, 98, 101, 102, 108

Plates

1. Ku K'ai-chih: The Nymph of the Lo River (section of scroll), Coll. Freer Gallery of Art, Washington, D.C.

2. Jataka Scene from Cave 110 at Tun Huang, Courtesy L. Warner

3. Sarcophagus with Stories of Filial Piety, Coll. Nelson Gallery of Art, Kansas City

4. Sacrificial House with Scenes of Filial Piety, Coll. Boston Museum of Fine Arts

5. Li Chao-tao (?): Travellers in Mountain Landscape, Coll. National Museum, Peking

6. Li Chao-tao (?): Travellers in Mountain Landscape (detail), Coll. National Museum, Peking

7. After Li Chao-tao: Ch'iu Ch'êng Palace, Coll. Boston Museum of Fine Arts

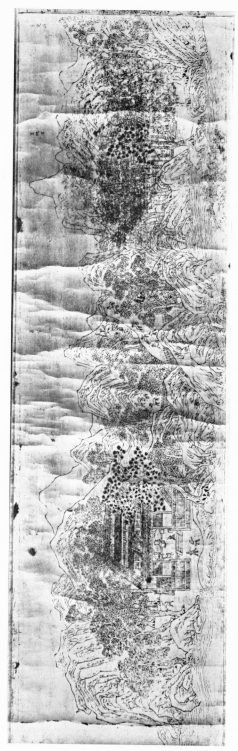

8. Wang Wei: Wang Ch'uan Scroll (section of scroll), Courtesy Chicago Natural History Museum

9. After Wang Wei: Winter Landscape, Coll. Freer Gallery of Art, Washington, D.C.

10. After Yang Shêng: Misty Landscape, Coll. Metropolitan
Museum of Art, New York

11. Anonymous artist: Winter Landscape, Coll. Palace Museum, Peking

12. Ching Hao: View of the K'uan-lu Mountains, Coll. Palace
Museum, Peking

13. Li Ch'êng: Travellers Among the Snowy
Hills, Coll. Boston Museum of Fine Arts

14. Li Ch'êng: Travellers Among the Snowy Hills (detail), Coll. Boston Museum of Fine Arts

15. Li Ch'êng: Reading the Stele, Coll. Osaka Museum of Art

16. Li Ch'êng (?): Buddhist Temple Amid Clearing Mountain
Peaks, Coll. Nelson Gallery of Art, Kansas City

17. Tung Yüan: A Clear Day in the Valley (section of scroll), Coll. Boston Museum of Fine Arts

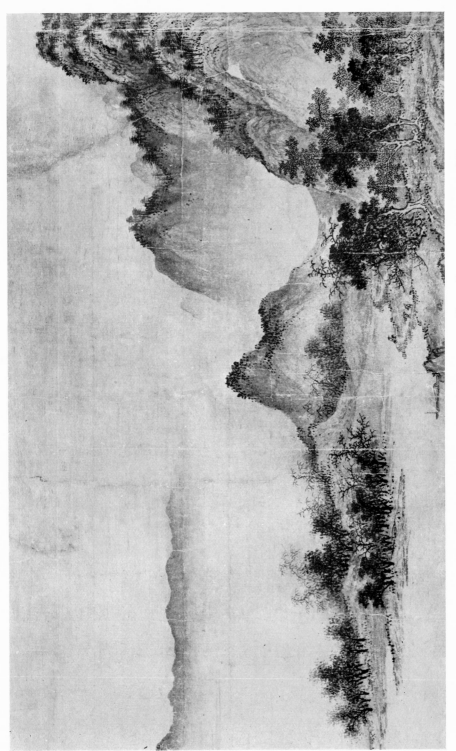

18. Tung Yüan: A Clear Day in the Valley (section of scroll), Coll. Boston Museum of Fine Arts

19. Tung Yüan: A Clear Day in the Valley (section of scroll), Coll. Boston Museum of Fine Arts

20. Tung Yüan: Cave of the Immortals, Coll. Palace Museum, Peking

21. Fan K'uan: Mountain Landscape, Coll. Palace Museum, Peking

22. Fan K'uan: Mountains with Palaces in Snow, Coll. Boston Museum of Fine Arts

23. Anonymous artist: Mountain Landscape, Coll. Nelson Gallery of
Art, Kansas City

24. Liao Tomb: Autumn Landscape, Palin, eastern Mongolia

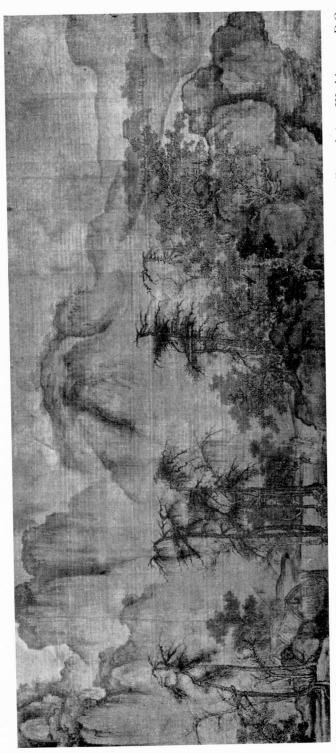

25. Kuo Hsi: An Autumn Day in the Valley of the Yellow River (section of scroll), Coll. Freer Gallery of Art, Washington, D.C.

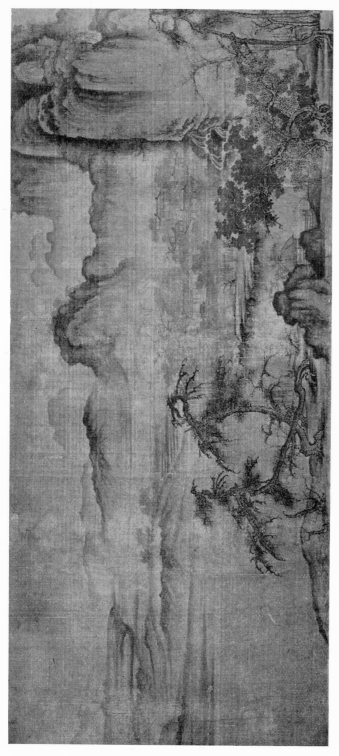

26. Kuo Hsi: An Autumn Day in the Valley of the Yellow River (section of scroll). Coll. Freer Gallery of Art, Washington, D.C.

27. Mi Fei: Misty Landscape, Coll. Freer Gallery of Art, Washington, D.C.

28. Mi Fei: Pine Trees and Mountains in Spring, Coll. Palace Museum, Peking

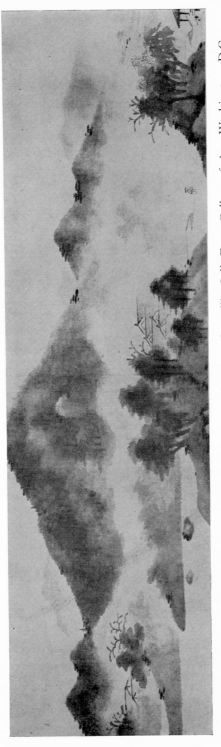

29. Mi Yu-jên: Misty Mountains and River Landscape (section of scroll), Coll. Freer Gallery of Art, Washington, D.C.

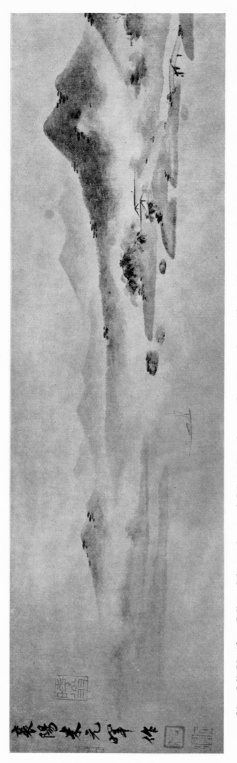

30. Mi Yu-jên: Misty Mountains and River Landscape (section of scroll), Coll. Freer Gallery of Art, Washington, D.C.

31. Anonymous artist: Tribute Horse, Coll. Metropolitan Museum of Art, New York

32. Li T'ang: Summer Landscape, Coll. Kōtō-in, Kyoto

33. Li T'ang: Summer Landscape (detail), Coll. Kōtō-in, Kyoto

34. Chao Po-chü: Entry of the First Emperor of the Han Dynasty into Kuan Chung (section of scroll), Coll. Boston Museum of Fine Arts

35. Chao Po-chü: Spring Morning at the Palace of the Han Emperors (section of scroll), Coll. Metropolitan Museum of Art, New York

36. Ma Yüan: Moonlit Night, Coll. Kuroda, Tokyo

37. Ma Yüan: Moonlit Night (detail), Coll. Kuroda, Tokyo

38. Ma Yüan: Bare Willows and Distant Mountains, Coll. Boston
Museum of Fine Arts

39. Ma Yüan: The Four Sages of Shang Shan (section of scroll), Coll. Cincinnati Art Museum

40. Hsia Kuei: Summer Landscape, Coll. Iwasaki, Tokyo

41. Hsia Kuei: Mountain and Lake Landscape (section of scroll), Coll. Nelson Gallery of Art, Kansas City

42. Hsia Kuei: Mountain and Lake Landscape (section of scroll), Coll. Nelson Gallery of Art, Kansas City

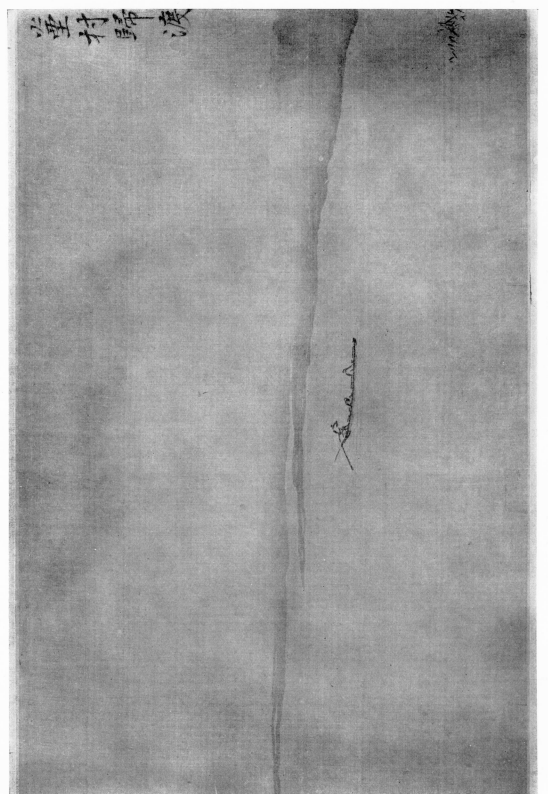

43. Hsia Kuei: Mountain and Lake Landscape (section of scroll), Coll. Nelson Gallery of Art, Kansas City

44. Hsia Kuei: Sailboat in the Rain, Coll. Boston Museum of Fine Arts

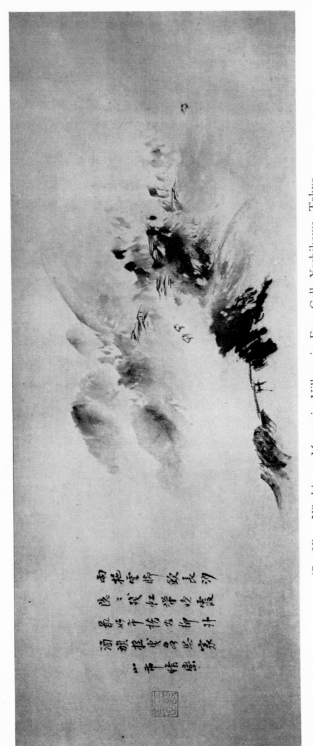

45. Ying Yü-chien: Mountain Village in Fog, Coll. Yoshikawa, Tokyo

46. Mu-ch'i: Eight Scenes of Hsiao-Hsiang (section), Coll. Masuda, Tokyo

47. Huang Kung-wang: Fu Ch'un Mountains, Coll. Mr.
P'ang Lai-chên, Shanghai

48. Huang Kung-wang (?): Mountain Landscape, Coll. Mr. Mathias Komor, New York

49. Wang Mêng: Landscape Scroll (section of scroll), Coll. Freer Gallery of Art,

50. Ni Tsan: Autumn Landscape, Coll. Freer Gallery of Art, Washington, D.C.

51. Hsü Pên: Interminable Rivers and Mountains (section of scroll), Coll. Freer Gallery of Art, Washington, D.C.

至大元年七月
廿六日 克恭

52. Kao K'o-kung: Rain in the Mountains, Coll. Detroit
Institute of Arts

53. Shên Chou: River Landscape (section of scroll), Coll. Freer Gallery of Art, Washington, D.C.

54. Shên Chou: Poet on a Mountain, Coll. Nelson Gallery of Art, Kansas City

55. Shên Chou: Poet on a Mountain (detail), Coll. Nelson Gallery of Art, Kansas City

56. Tai Chin: Autumn River Landscape with Fishing Boats (section of scroll), Coll. Freer Gallery of Art, Washington, D.C.

57. Tai Chin: Autumn River Landscape with Fishing Boats (section of scroll), Coll. Freer Gallery of Art, Washington, D.C.

58. Tai Chin: River Landscape (section of scroll), Coll. Freer Gallery of Art, Washington, D.C.

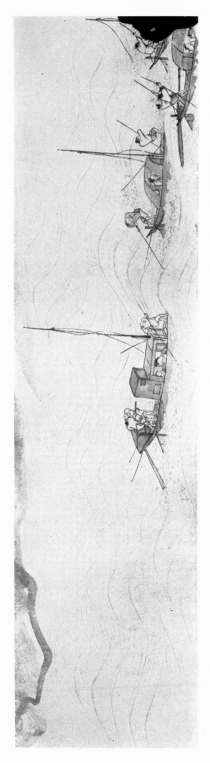

59. Tai Chin: River Landscape (section of scroll), Coll. Freer Gallery of Art, Washington, D.C.

60. Wên Chêng-ming: Landscape Scroll (section of scroll), Coll. Freer Gallery of Art, Washington, D.C.

61. T'ang Yin: Mountain Landscape (section of scroll), Coll. Freer Gallery of Art, Washington, D.C.

62. Ch'iu Ying: Garden Feast, Coll. Chion-in, Kyoto

63. Wang Hui: Mount Fu Ch'un (section of scroll), Coll. Freer Gallery of Art, Washington, D.C.

64. Wang Hui: Mount Fu Ch'un (section of scroll), Coll. Freer Gallery of Art, Washington, D.C.

65. Shih-t'ao: Mountain Landscape, Coll. Nü Wa Chai, China

66. Pa-ta Shan-jên: Rocks and Fish, Private Collection, New York

67. Yüan Chiang: Carts on a Winding Mountain Road, Coll.
Nelson Gallery of Art, Kansas City

68. Anonymous artist: Sages in a Landscape (section of scroll), Coll. Freer Gallery of Art, Washington, D.C.

69. Wang Cheng-kuo: Landscape Scroll, Coll.
Mr. Mathias Komor, New York

70. Wang Chi-ch'üan: Rocks and Water, Coll. the artist, New York

71. Jataka Scene from Tamamushi Shrine, Coll. Hōryūji, Nara

72. Kako Genzai Inga Kyō (section of scroll), Coll. Jōhōrendai-ji, Kyoto

73. Plectrum Guard of Biwa, Coll. Shōsō-in, Nara

74. Hemp Cloth with Landscape (detail), Coll. Shōsō-in, Nara

75. Senzui Byōbu, Coll. Tō-ji, Kyoto

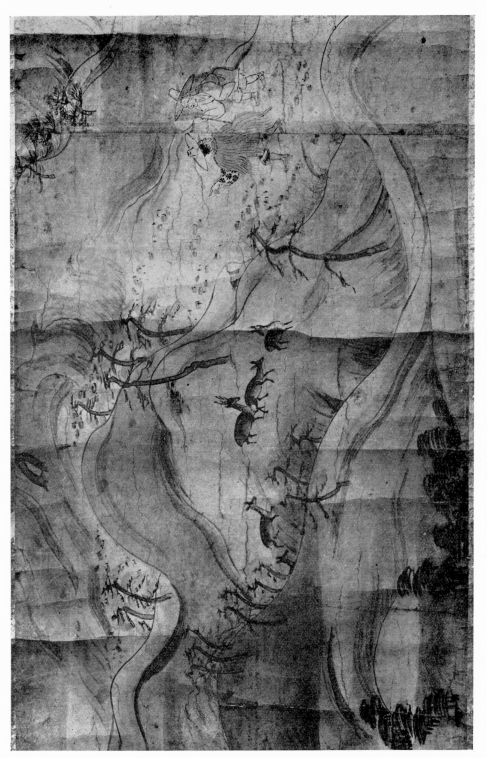

76. Shigisan Engi Scroll (section), Coll. Chōgosonshi-ji, Nara

77. Senzui Byōbu, (section), Coll Jingo-ji, Kyoto

78. Nachi Waterfall, Coll. Nezu Museum, Tokyo

79. Shūbun: Landscape Scroll, Coll. Fujiwara, Tokyo

80. Sesshū: Landscape Scroll (section), Coll. Mōri, Tokyo

81. Sesshū: Landscape, Coll. National Museum, Tokyo

82. Sōami: Landscape, Coll. Daisen-in, Daitoku-ji, Kyoto

83. Motonobu: Priest Ling-yün Viewing Peach Blossoms, Coll.
National Museum, Tokyo

84. Sesson: Landscape, Coll. Nomura, Kyoto

85. Kano Eitoku: Hawk on Pine Screen, Coll. University of Arts, Tokyo

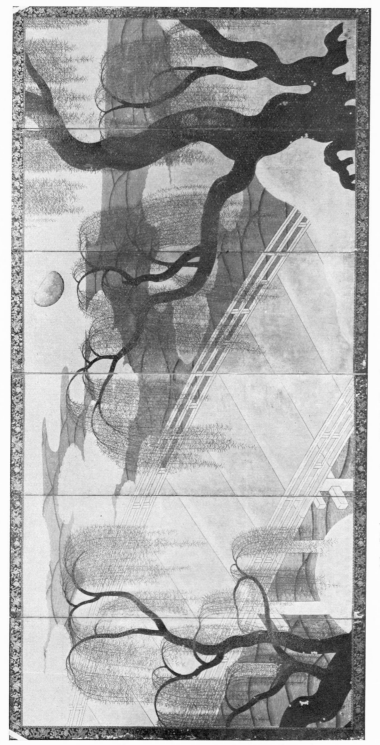

86. Unknown artist: Uji Bridge Screen, Private Collection, Tokyo

87. Kaihō Yūshō: Screen with Fishing Nets, Coll. National Museum, Tokyo

88. Hasegawa Tōhaku: Screen with Pines, Coll. National Museum, Tokyo

89. Kano Naonobu: Landscape Screen, Coll. National Museum, Tokyo

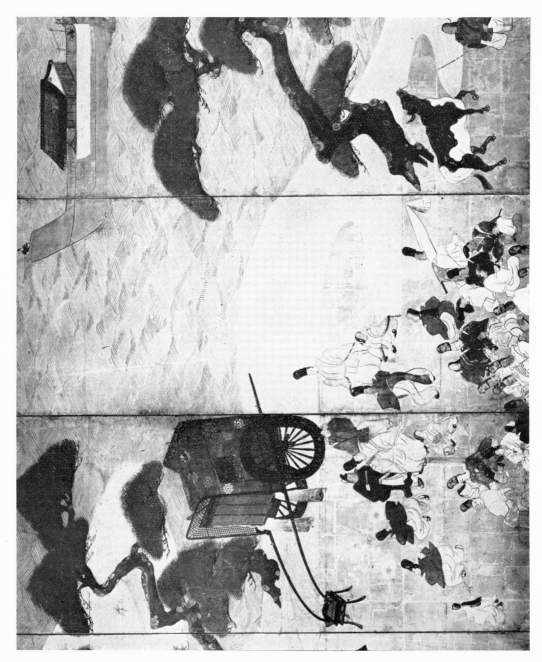

90. Sōtatsu: Genji Monogatari Screen (detail), Coll. Seikadō Bunko, Tokyo

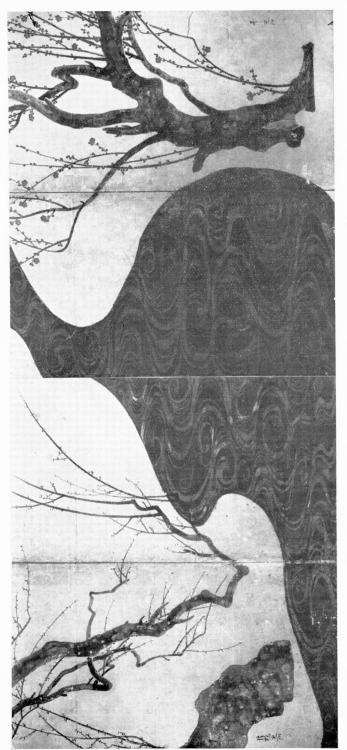

91. Ogata Kōrin: Plum Tree Screen, Coll. Tsugaru, Tokyo

課農便
山甸四面總玲瓏綠野青疇一望中偓兀課農
農力盡何曾妨却讀書王

92. Ikeno Taiga: Convenience of Farming, Coll. Kawabata, Kamakura

93. Gyokudō: Mountain Landscape, Coll. Yamaguchi, Kyoto

94. Maruyama Ōkyo: Hozu River Screen (detail), Coll. Nishimura, Kyoto

95. Goshun: Snow Scene Screen (section), Coll. National Museum, Tokyo

96. Shiba Kōkan: Shinobazu-no-Ike, Coll. National Museum, Tokyo

97. Hokusai: Fuji in Clear Weather, Coll. National Museum, Tokyo

98. Hokusai: Fujimihara, Coll. National Museum, Tokyo

99. Hiroshige: Shower at Atake Bridge, Coll. National Museum, Tokyo

100. Hiroshige: Fuji at Yui, Coll. National Museum, Tokyo

東
海
道
五
拾
三
次
之
内

亀
山

101. Hiroshige: Snow at Kameyama, Coll. National Museum, Tokyo